BUSINESS ISSUES, COMPETITION AND ENTREPRENEURSHIP

FEDERAL CONTRACTING WITH TRIBAL FIRMS AND SMALL BUSINESS ADMINISTRATION OVERSIGHT OF ALASKA NATIVE CORPORATIONS

ASSESSMENTS

BUSINESS ISSUES, COMPETITION AND ENTREPRENEURSHIP

Additional books in this series can be found on Nova's website under the Series tab.

Additional e-books in this series can be found on Nova's website under the eBooks tab.

BUSINESS ISSUES, COMPETITION AND ENTREPRENEURSHIP

FEDERAL CONTRACTING WITH TRIBAL FIRMS AND SMALL BUSINESS ADMINISTRATION OVERSIGHT OF ALASKA NATIVE CORPORATIONS

ASSESSMENTS

GAIL NELSON
EDITOR

nova publishers
New York

Library of Congress Cataloging-in-Publication Data

ISBN: 978-1-53610-367-0

Published by Nova Science Publishers, Inc. † New York

CONTENTS

Preface		**vii**
Chapter 1	Federal Contracting: Monitoring and Oversight of Tribal 8(a) Firms Need Attention *United States Government Accountability Office*	**1**
Chapter 2	Alaska Native Corporations: Oversight Weaknesses Continue to Limit SBA's Ability to Monitor Compliance with 8(a) Program Requirements *United States Government Accountability Office*	**65**
Index		**141**

PREFACE

Tribal firms—those owned by Alaska Native Corporations, Native Hawaiian Organizations, and Indian tribes—are afforded special advantages within the Small Business Administration's (SBA) 8(a) business development program. This book identifies trends in government 8(a) contracting with tribal firms; determines why the government awarded sole-source contracts to tribal 8(a) firms and the methods used to make price determinations; assesses the procuring agencies' oversight of contracts for compliance with subcontracting requirements; and examines SBA's new 8(a) regulation, intended to clarify program rules, to determine how the changes could affect oversight of tribal 8(a) firms.

In: Federal Contracting
Editor: Gail Nelson
ISBN: 978-1-53610-367-0

Chapter 1

FEDERAL CONTRACTING: MONITORING AND OVERSIGHT OF TRIBAL 8(A) FIRMS NEED ATTENTION*

United States Government Accountability Office

WHY GAO DID THIS STUDY

Tribal firms—those owned by Alaska Native Corporations, Native Hawaiian Organizations, and Indian tribes—are afforded special advantages within the Small Business Administration's (SBA) 8(a) business development program. GAO was asked to (1) identify trends in government 8(a) contracting with tribal firms; (2) determine why the government awarded sole-source contracts to tribal 8(a) firms and the methods used to make price determinations; (3) assess the procuring agencies' oversight of contracts for compliance with subcontracting requirements; and (4) examine SBA's new 8(a) regulation, intended to clarify program rules, to determine how the changes could affect oversight of tribal 8(a) firms. GAO reviewed non-generalizable samples of 87 contracts (based on dollar value and location) and 62 tribal 8(a) firms' SBA files and spoke with SBA headquarters and district officials as well as officials from 9 agencies.

---

* This is an edited, reformatted and augmented version of the United States Government Accountability Office publication, GAO-12-84, dated January 2012.

WHAT GAO RECOMMENDS

GAO recommends that the Office of Federal Procurement Policy (OFPP) amend acquisition regulations and provide guidance (including data collection) on monitoring the limits on subcontracting. OFPP generally agreed with the recommendations. GAO's recommendations also include that SBA include specific capabilities in its 8(a) database to improve tribal 8(a) tracking and that it examine tribal participation to determine whether certain practices align with the 8(a) program's business development goal. SBA questioned GAO's methodology, which GAO continues to believe is appropriate, but did not address GAO's recommendations.

WHAT GAO FOUND

Federal dollars obligated to tribal 8(a) firms grew from $2.1 billion in fiscal year 2005 to $5.5 billion in 2010, a greater percentage increase than non-tribal 8(a) obligations (160 percent versus 45 percent). Obligations to 8(a) firms owned by Alaska Native Corporations (ANC) represented the majority of tribal obligations every year during the period, rising to $4.7 billion in 2010. While tribal 8(a) firms comprised 6.2 percent of total 8(a) firms, their obligations accounted for almost a third of total 8(a) obligations in fiscal year 2010. Over the 6 years, the percentage of competitively awarded obligations to tribal 8(a) firms rose; however, sole-source contracts remained the primary source of growth, representing at least 75 percent of all tribal 8(a) obligations in a given year.

Consistent with GAO's 2006 review of ANC 8(a) contracting, contracting officials said that awarding contracts to tribal firms under the 8(a) program allows officials to award sole-source contracts for any value quickly, easily, and legally, and helps agencies meet their small business goals. However, the officials added that the program offices' push for awarding follow-on contracts to the same firm also plays a role. GAO's review of noncompetitive tribal 8(a) contracts shows the methods used to determine price reasonableness in a sole-source environment. In some cases, when agencies moved away from sole-source tribal 8(a) contracts toward competition, agency officials estimated savings as a result.

To ensure that 8(a) firms do not pass along the benefits of their contracts to their subcontractors, regulations limit the amount of work that can be performed by the subcontractors. Of the 87 contracts in GAO's review, 71 had subcontractors. GAO found that required monitoring of limitations on subcontracting by procuring agencies was not routinely occurring. Similar to what GAO reported in 2006, some contracting officers do not understand that ensuring compliance is their responsibility under partnership agreements with SBA, and the regulations do not make this clear. Further, agency officials did not know how to monitor subcontracting limitations, particularly for indefinite-quantity contracts, as the data are not readily available. Not monitoring the limits on subcontracting can pose a major risk that an improper amount of work is being done by large firms.

In March 2011, SBA revised 8(a) regulations to clarify program rules, correct misinterpretations, and address program issues. Although a positive step, SBA will have difficulty enforcing new regulations pertaining to tribal 8(a) follow-on contracts and joint ventures given the information currently available. SBA told GAO it is currently in the process of developing the requirements for a new 8(a) tracking database. Further, the new regulations do not address some issues GAO has previously raised, such as ANC 8(a) firms under the same parent corporation generating a majority of revenue in the same line of business. SBA regulations do not allow a tribal organization to have more than one 8(a) subsidiary perform most of its work under the same primary business line. GAO also discusses practices that highlight how some tribal 8(a) firms operate, in effect, as large businesses because of their parent corporation's backing and interconnectedness with sister subsidiaries. SBA has not reviewed these practices to determine whether they are congruent with the business development purpose of the 8(a) program.

ABBREVIATIONS

ANC	Alaska Native Corporation
ANCSA	Alaska Native Claims Settlement Act
BOA	basic ordering agreement
DCAA	Defense Contract Audit Agency
DOD	Department of Defense
DUNS	Data Universal Numbering System
FAR	Federal Acquisition Regulation
FPDS-NG	Federal Procurement Data System-Next Generation
GSA	U.S. General Services Administration
NAICS	North American Industry Classification System

NHO	Native Hawaiian Organization
OFPP	Office of Federal Procurement Policy
OMB	Office of Management and Budget
SBA	Small Business Administration

***

January 31, 2012

Congressional Requesters:

The federal government obligates hundreds of billions of dollars in contracts for goods and services each year—about $537 billion in fiscal year 2010. That year, about $18.5 billion was obligated to firms participating in the Small Business Administration's (SBA) 8(a) program. The 8(a) program is one of the federal government's primary means for developing small businesses owned by socially and economically disadvantaged individuals. Congress has repeatedly emphasized in legislation that the purpose of the 8(a) program is business development, with a goal of enabling these businesses to compete on an equal basis in the mainstream American economy. Over two decades ago, Congress expanded participation in the 8(a) program to include not just firms owned by disadvantaged individuals, but also firms owned by tribal entities. In this report, "tribal entities" refers to Alaska Native Corporations (ANC), Indian tribes, and Native Hawaiian Organizations (NHO). We use the term "tribal 8(a) firm" to refer to a firm that is majority owned by an ANC, Indian tribe, or NHO.

Firms owned by tribal entities have been afforded special advantages in the 8(a) program. For example, they can receive sole-source 8(a) contracts for any amount, whereas sole-source awards to other 8(a) firms generally must be made under certain competitive dollar thresholds ($6.5 million for manufacturing or $4 million for all other acquisitions). ANCs, created in 1971 through the Alaska Native Claims Settlement Act (ANCSA), were established to distribute land and monetary benefits to Alaska Native shareholders in lieu of a reservation system.[1] Relevant legislation defines the term Indian tribes to include bands, nations, or other organized groups of communities of Indians, which are recognized as eligible for the special programs and services provided by the United States because of their status as Indians. NHOs are not-for-profit community service organizations controlled by Native Hawaiians whose business activities are to principally benefit Native Hawaiians. These tribal entities generally provide, to varying extents, economic and community development for their native populations through different programs.

In a 2006 report, we noted that the legislative history leading to the procurement advantages for ANCs was sparse and confusing.[2] We also reported on the challenge SBA officials cited in overseeing ANC activity in the 8(a) program. The officials attributed this challenge to the fact that the program's business development goals can be in conflict with ANCs' charter under ANCSA—economic and community development for Alaska Natives. We made a number of recommendations, focused on the need for improved SBA oversight of the special advantages afforded to ANCs under the 8(a) program. The Small Business Act does not provide tribal entities a purpose in the 8(a) program that is different from the program's stated goal of business development. In fact, in a 1989 revision to the 8(a) program regulations, SBA stated that the 8(a) program is intended to be used exclusively for business development purposes to help small businesses owned and controlled by socially and economically disadvantaged individuals, Indian tribes, ANCs, and NHOs to compete on an equal basis in the mainstream of the American economy.[3] We also reported in 2006 that agencies were not effectively monitoring compliance with required percentages of work to be performed by 8(a) firms versus their subcontractors. While our 2006 report focused on 8(a) firms owned by ANCs, the scope of this report includes 8(a) firms owned by Indian tribes and NHOs as well.

SBA revised the 8(a) regulations, effective in March 2011, to clarify and refine certain provisions in the program, with some revisions specifically focused on tribal participation. Also in March 2011, the Federal Acquisition Regulation (FAR) was amended,[4] on an interim basis, to implement a provision in the National Defense Authorization Act for Fiscal Year 2010 that required a written justification prior to awarding sole- source 8(a) contracts over \$20 million[5] Previously, no justification was required for any dollar amount for 8(a) contracts, including those awarded to tribal 8(a) firms.

In response to your request, we (1) identified trends in federal obligations under 8(a) contracts with tribal firms; (2) determined the reasons federal agencies awarded sole-source contracts to tribal 8(a) firms and the methods used to make price determinations; (3) assessed the procuring agencies' oversight of tribal 8(a) contracts for compliance with subcontracting requirements; and (4) examined SBA's new 8(a) regulations to determine how the changes could affect oversight of tribal firms and the extent to which previously identified problems are addressed. During the course of our work, we also discussed with procuring agency officials the potential impact of the recent FAR requirement for written justifications for sole-source 8(a) awards over $20 million. This requirement was not applicable to the contracts we reviewed. We evaluated the administration of the tribal 8(a) program; the scope of our work did not include an evaluation of the program's merits.

To identify trends in 8(a) contracting with tribal firms, we analyzed data from the Federal Procurement Data System-Next Generation (FPDS-NG) for fiscal years 2005 through 2010 (the last year of complete information at the time of our review). We found the FPDS-NG data fields that identify firms owned by ANCs, NHOs, and Indian tribes to be unreliable because these data were not available during the entire time period. We therefore obtained from SBA tribal 8(a) firms' Data Universal Numbering System (DUNS) numbers and used this information to obtain the FPDS-NG data, which we determined was sufficiently reliable to identify trends in tribal 8(a) contracting. To address our second and third objectives, we used a stratified purposeful, selected sampling approach to identify 87 contracts for review.[6] This nonprobability sample included contracts over the competitive 8(a) threshold amounts ($6.5 million for manufacturing and $4 million for other acquisitions), focusing on those with large dollar value obligations in fiscal year 2009 (the latest data available at the time we selected our contract sample). We also focused on contracting activities that had higher levels of sole-source tribal 8(a) activity. The majority of the contracts in our sample (62) were awarded by defense agencies, and 25 were awarded by civilian agencies, including the departments of Agriculture, Energy, Health and Human Services, Homeland Security, Justice, Labor, and State, and the Social Security Administration. Most (75) of the contracts were with ANC 8(a) firms; 10 were with firms owned by Indian tribes and 2 were with firms owned by NHOs. Of the 87 contracts, 7 were competitively awarded, and 79 were sole-source procurements. For the one remaining contract we could not confirm whether it was awarded competitively or not because the entire pre-award file was missing. We reviewed the contract files and spoke with contracting and program officials and small business advocates at the agency locations. The results of our contract file analysis are not generalizable to the population of tribal 8(a) contracts.

To address the potential effect of the new SBA regulations on oversight of tribal firms and the extent to which previously identified problems were addressed, we visited SBA headquarters as well as district offices in Anchorage, AK; Philadelphia, PA; and Washington, DC. We also spoke with

SBA district officials in Hawaii, New Mexico, and Oklahoma. We selected these particular district offices primarily based on their relatively higher level of involvement with tribal 8(a) firms. In addition to the 87 contract files we reviewed, we also reviewed a sample of 62 SBA files for tribal 8(a) firms' application information, annual reviews, and business plans. In selecting the firms for this portion of our work, we focused on those that had relatively high representation in our contract sample as well as those that had relatively low representation. The results of our review of the firms' SBA files are not generalizable to the universe of tribal 8(a) firms. We did not assess the extent to which benefits from tribal 8(a) contracts flow to the parent entity.

To understand the potential impact of the new FAR requirement for written justifications of 8(a) sole-source awards over $20 million, we reviewed the FAR and public comments on the new rule: interviewed agency small business advocates, Office of Federal Procurement Policy (OFPP) officials, and contracting officers for the contracts we reviewed; and drew from the findings in our prior report on ANC 8(a) contracting.[7] The Administrator of OFPP serves as chair of the Federal Acquisition Regulatory Council; the council oversees development and maintenance of the FAR.

Appendix I contains more information on our scope and methodology. We conducted this performance audit from October 2010 to January 2012 in accordance with generally accepted government auditing standards. Those standards require that we plan and perform the audit to obtain sufficient, appropriate evidence to provide a reasonable basis for our findings and conclusions based on our audit objectives. We believe that the evidence obtained provides a reasonable basis for our findings and conclusions based on our audit objectives.

BACKGROUND

ANCs, Indian tribes and NHOs—i.e., the parent entities of tribal 8(a) firms—can be large, with worldwide operations and revenues in the hundreds of millions of dollars. They can own 8(a) and non-8(a) subsidiaries and sometimes form complicated corporate structures. Figure 1 illustrates a notional corporate structure of an ANC with a holding company—a non-8(a) subsidiary that provides shared administrative services to other subsidiaries for a fee. The figure depicts a mix of 8(a) and non-8(a) subsidiaries that may be only partly owned by the ANC.

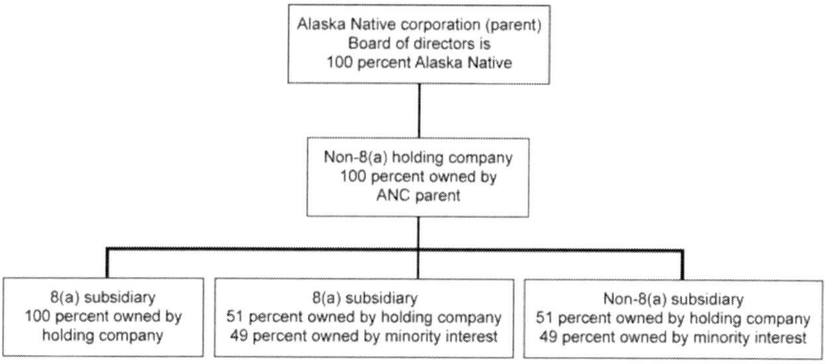

Note: Only the 8(a) subsidiaries would be eligible for 8(a) contracts.
Source: GAO analysis.

Figure 1. Notional ANC with Holding Company and Multiple Subsidiaries.

According to SBA, in fiscal year 2010, there were over 8,400 firms in the 8(a) program, 354 of which were owned by a tribal entity. For any firm (including tribal firms) to be eligible to participate in the 8(a) program, it must qualify as small under a primary industry size standard as measured by the number of employees or average revenues from the previous 3 years. In addition, the firm must be, among other things, majority-owned by one or more socially and economically disadvantaged individuals or a qualified entity, such as a tribal entity. Firms approved as 8(a) participants can receive business development assistance from SBA and are eligible to receive contracts that agencies offer to SBA for the 8(a) program. All 8(a) firms, including tribal 8(a) firms, are subject to a 9-year limit on participation in the 8(a) program. During the last 5 years in the program, known as a transitional period, firms are required to obtain a certain percentage of non-8(a) revenue to demonstrate their progress in developing a viable business that is not solely reliant on the 8(a) program. SBA's district offices are responsible for tracking this business mix on an annual basis. If a firm does not meet its required business mix during one of the last 5 years, SBA invokes a plan of remedial action for the next year, in which the firm is to report to SBA on its progress. Until the required mix is demonstrated, the firm will generally not be eligible for sole-source 8(a) contracts.

Congress has provided tribal 8(a) firms with distinct advantages over other 8(a) businesses, in addition to the ability to receive sole-source 8(a) contracts for any amount. In some cases, there are also differences among the advantages provided to firms owned by ANCs, Indian tribes, and NHOs. Table 1 provides more details.

Table 1. Differences in Requirements for Tribal 8(a) Firms and Other 8(a) Firms

Requirement	Firms owned by an ANC	Firms owned by an Indian Tribe	Firms owned by an NHO	Other 8(a) firms
Number of firms a participant may own	No limit as long as each business is in a different primary industry.			Only one in a lifetime.
Size determination for eligibility in 8(a) program	Other affiliated companies not considered in size determination; however, the SBA Administrator may find the existence of affiliation if, for example, SBA determines that the tribal 8(a) firm or firms have a substantial unfair competitive advantage within an industry.			For-profit, nonprofit, domestic, and foreign affiliates considered in size determination.
Competitive threshold	No threshold. Procurements need not be competed before being accepted on a sole-source basis.		No threshold for DOD contracts only. DOD procurements need not be competed before being accepted on a sole-source basis.	Can receive sole-source contracts for up to \$6.5 million for manufacturing or \$4 million for all other acquisitions.
Dollar limits on amount of sole-source 8(a) contracts	No limits on the amount of sole-source contracts.			May not receive sole- source 8(a) contract awards if the combined total of competitive and sole source 8(a) contracts received is above (1) \$100 million where a firm's size is based on its number of employees, or, (2) the lesser of \$100 million or five times the size standard for the industry where a firm's size is based on revenues.[a]
Demonstration of social and economic disadvantage	Deemed in legislation as socially and economically disadvantaged.	Defined as socially disadvantaged, but must demonstrate that the tribe is economically disadvantaged in connection with the	Deemed socially disadvantaged but must establish economic disadvantage and that its business activities principally benefit Native	Must (1) be a member of a group deemed as socially disadvantaged or prove social disadvantage by meeting certain standards and (2) must prove economic disadvantage.

Table 1. (Continued)

Requirement	Firms owned by an ANC	Firms owned by an Indian Tribe	Firms owned by an NHO	Other 8(a) firms
		application for one tribally-owned firm.[b] The tribe need not reestablish its economic disadvantage to have other businesses it owns certified for 8(a) participation, unless requested to do so by SBA.	Hawaiians. Economic disadvantage for an NHO is determined when the majority of an NHO's members—or if no members, the board of directors—qualify as economically disadvantaged individuals. Economic disadvantage must be determined for every 8(a) applicant.	
Management background	President/chief executive officer need not be a disadvantaged individual.	Management and daily operations must be controlled by the tribe. The concern may be controlled by the tribe through one or more individuals who possess sufficient management experience to run the firm or through management, which can be a non-tribal member.[c]	President/chief executive officer need not be a disadvantaged individual.	President/chief executive officer must be a disadvantaged individual.
Potential for success	(1) Must be in business in primary industry classification for at least 2 years before 8(a) application date; or (2) generally, the individuals who will manage and control the daily business operations of the firm have substantial technical and management experience; the applicant has successful past performance on contracts from government and non-government sources in its primary			Must be in business in primary industry classification for at least 2 years before 8(a) application date.

Requirement	Firms owned by an ANC	Firms owned by an Indian Tribe	Firms owned by an NHO	Other 8(a) firms
	industry, and the applicant has adequate capital to sustain its operations and carry out its business plan as a participant; or (3) the tribal entity made a firm written commitment to support the operations of the applicant concern and it has the financial ability to do so.			SBA can waive the requirement if certain conditions are met, such as substantial business experience, adequate capital, and past success on contracts.

Source: GAO analysis of SBA 8(a) laws and regulations.

[a] 8(a) contracts awarded under $100,000 will not be considered in the $100 million limit.

[b] This includes consideration of available data such as present tribal unemployment rate, the per capita income of tribal members, and percentage of local Indian population below the poverty level.

[c] Management is provided by either (1) committees, teams, or Board of Directors controlled by at least one economically disadvantaged tribe member; or (2) non-tribal members if the tribe can hire and fire those individuals, retains control of all management decisions, and a written plan exists which shows how tribal members will develop managerial skills sufficient to manage the 8(a) firm or similar tribally- owned firms in the future.

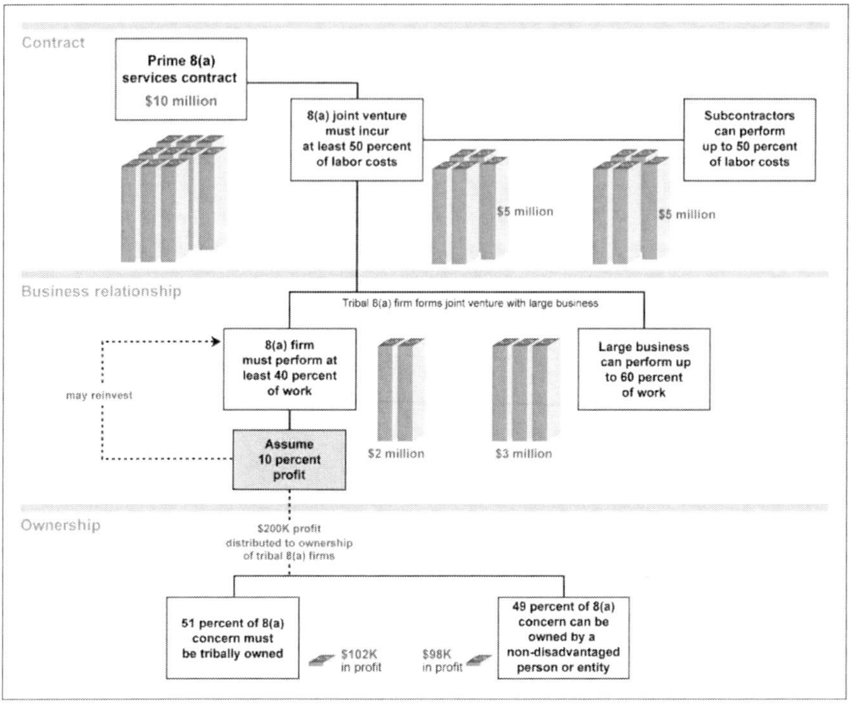

Source: GAO analysis of SBA regulations.

Notes: In our example, the joint venture is unpopulated—meaning it merely exists through a written agreement and uses the employees of the firms in the joint venture. The profits from an unpopulated joint venture are distributed commensurate with the work performed; thus, in this example the 8(a) firm receives 10 percent in profit from the 40 percent of the work it performed.

For 8(a) construction contracts, the prime contractor must incur at least 15 percent of the personnel costs with its own employees. Thus, if our illustrative example above were a construction contract, the tribe that owns a 51 percent interest in the firm would receive $31,000 in profit distribution.

Figure 2. Flow of Work and Profits As Allowed in the 8(a) Program under an Illustrative Contract for Services.

For tribal 8(a) firms, SBA has specific oversight responsibility for

- accepting the firm into the program, which includes ensuring that the tribal entity owning the firm does not have more than one 8(a) firm in the same primary line of business, defined by a North American Industry Classification System (NAICS) code[8] and

- annually reviewing 8(a) firms to track their progress in the 8(a) program, including their mix of 8(a) and non-8(a) revenue in the last 5 years in the program and any changes to the firms' business targets, objectives, and goals.

The procuring agency offers, and SBA may accept, a procuring agency's requirement into the 8(a) program either as a competitive procurement— to be competed among all eligible 8(a) firms—or as a sole-source procurement. The agency's offer letter must identify the requirement, any procurement history, the estimated dollar amount, and NAICS code, among other things.[9] Before accepting a procurement as an 8(a) sole- source contract, SBA is to verify the proposed firm's size status to ensure that it qualifies as small under the identified NAICS code. Once accepted into the program, 8(a) firms may pursue contracts in additional lines of work, called secondary NAICS codes. Once a requirement is awarded as an 8(a) contract, it must remain in the 8(a) program unless the procuring agency decides it would like to fulfill the follow-on requirement outside of the program and requests approval from SBA to do so. Procuring agency contracting officers also have responsibilities under the 8(a) program. For all of the agencies in our review, SBA has delegated responsibility for contract administration to the contracting officers through partnership agreements.[10] These responsibilities include, for example, ensuring compliance with the limitations on subcontracting requirements under 8(a) contracts.

SBA's 8(a) program regulations allow for involvement of other businesses and non-disadvantaged individuals as a way of helping the 8(a) business grow and develop. For example, 8(a) firms can hire outside agents to assist them in obtaining 8(a) contracts; however, SBA's revised regulations now prohibit agreements in which agents receive a percentage of the contract value as compensation for their assistance. In addition, large businesses can create a mentor-protégé joint venture with an 8(a) firm to win 8(a) prime contracts or can act as a subcontractor under an 8(a) contract.[11] Certain limitations apply regarding the percentage of labor costs that 8(a) firms and non-8(a) partners may incur under service and construction contracts. For service contracts with subcontracting activity, the 8(a) firm must incur at least 50 percent of the personnel costs with its own employees (15 percent for construction contracts). Further, a non-disadvantaged individual can own up to a 49 percent interest in an 8(a) firm, retaining his or her percentage of ownership in the profits the firm generates. These arrangements with other businesses or non-disadvantaged individuals can result in a relatively small percentage of contract profits being retained by the tribal entity that owns the 8(a) firm. Figure 2 is an illustrative example of how these arrangements could occur when a tribal 8(a) firm forms a joint venture with a large business under the mentor-protégé program, as allowed by SBA regulations.

In 2006, we reported that ANCs used the 8(a) program as one of many sources of revenue (which could include revenue generated outside of government contracts) to provide benefits to their shareholders.[12] We also found that there was no explicit link between the revenues ANCs generated from the 8(a) program and the benefits they provided to shareholders, because ANCs only tracked benefits generated from their consolidated revenue sources. The recently revised 8(a) regulations require tribal 8(a) firms to report annually to SBA on the benefits they are providing their members or community from their participation in the 8(a) program.

Obligations to Tribal 8(a) Firms Have Grown Steadily, with Most under Sole-Source Contracts

From fiscal year 2005 through 2010, federal dollars obligated to tribal 8(a) firms grew from $2.1 billion to $5.5 billion. Obligations to 8(a) firms owned by ANCs—which represented the majority of these tribal obligations during each fiscal year—rose steadily, from $1.9 billion to $4.7 billion. Obligations to 8(a) firms owned by Indian tribes and NHOs also grew steadily during this time frame, to $690 million and $109 million, respectively, in fiscal year 2010. Total 8(a) obligations (to tribal and non- tribal 8(a) firms) increased from $11.3 billion to $18.8 billion during the six-year period. Obligations to tribal 8(a) firms represented a 160 percent increase over this time, while obligations to non-tribal 8(a) firms increased 45 percent. Figure 3 shows the growth of non-tribal and tribal 8(a) obligations.

Tribal firms represented a very small percentage of all 8(a) firms, but accounted for almost 30 percent of 8(a) obligations—about $5.5 billion— in fiscal year 2010, as shown in Table 2.

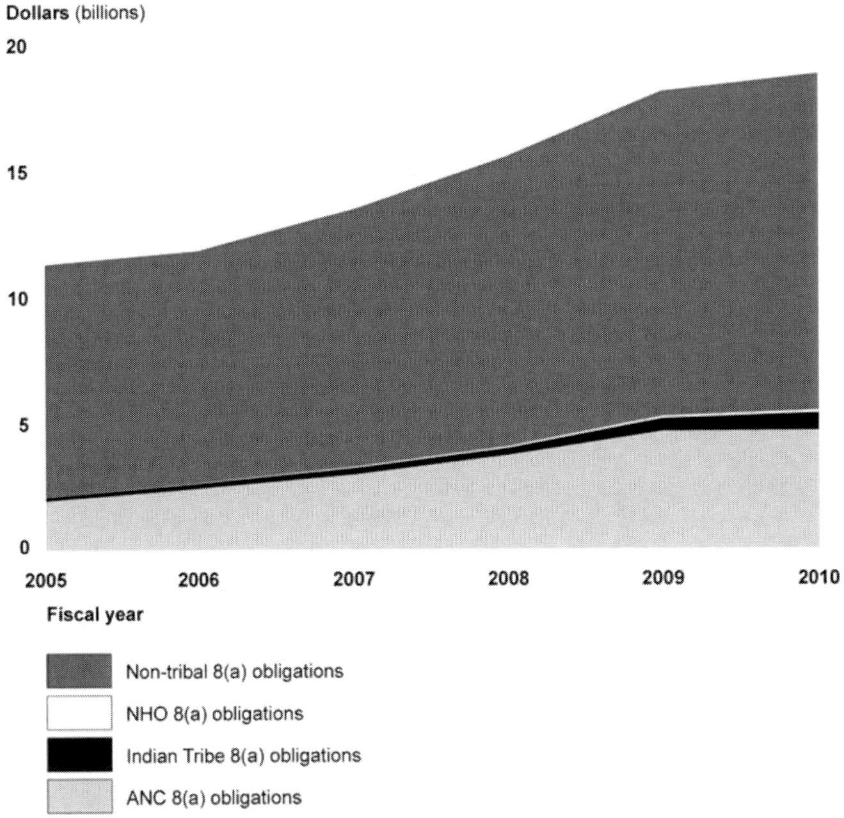

Source: GAO analysis based on information from FPDS-NG.
Note: Obligation amounts are inflation adjusted to 2010 dollars.

Figure 3. Obligations to Non-Tribal and Tribal 8(a) Firms, Fiscal Years 2005 through 2010 (dollars in billions).

The percentage of obligations under competitively awarded tribal 8(a) contracts increased from fiscal year 2005 to 2010. In fiscal year 2010, sole-source obligations to ANC 8(a) firms decreased slightly, for the first time since 2005. Table 3 compares the percentage of obligations under competitively awarded contracts for ANC, Indian tribe, and NHO 8(a) firms in fiscal year 2005 and 2010.

Table 2. Number of Tribal and Non-tribal 8(a) Firms and Obligations in Fiscal Year 2010

	Number of 8 (a) firms	Percentage of total number of 8(a) firms	8(a) obligations (in millions)	Percentage of FY 10 8(a) obligations
Non-tribal 8(a) firms	5,340	93.8	$13,310	70.8
Tribal 8(a) firms	353	6.2	5,480	29.2
Total	**5,693**	**100**	**18,790**	**100**

Source: GAO analysis of FPDS-NG data.

Table 3. Percentage of Obligations under Competitively Awarded Contracts to Tribal 8(a) Firms for Fiscal Year 2005 and 2010

8(a) firms owned by	Fiscal year 2005 (percent)	Fiscal year 2010 (percent)
ANC	14.8	21.8
Indian tribe	10.2	18.1
NHO	4.2	26

Source: GAO analysis of FPDS-NG data.

Even with this increase in obligations under competitively awarded contracts to tribal 8(a) firms, sole-source contracts still accounted for at least 75 percent of all tribal 8(a) obligations annually. In terms of obligations, in fiscal year 2010, sole-source awards to tribal 8(a) firms accounted for $4.3 billion of the total $5.5 billion in tribal 8(a) obligations. Figure 4 shows the breakdown of sole-source and competitive 8(a) obligations for tribal and non-tribal 8(a) firms from fiscal years 2005 through 2010.

As shown in figure 4, the percentage of competitive obligations for non-tribal 8(a) firms—about 45 percent in fiscal year 2010—still far outpaces those of tribal 8(a) firms.

Further, our analysis of FPDS-NG obligation data for new sole source awards under the 8(a) program, issued from fiscal years 2005 through 2010, reveals that for both tribal and non-tribal 8(a) firms, obligations on sole-source 8(a) awards increased during the last month of each fiscal year.[13] Figure 5 shows the dramatic spike in 8(a) obligations in September of each year.

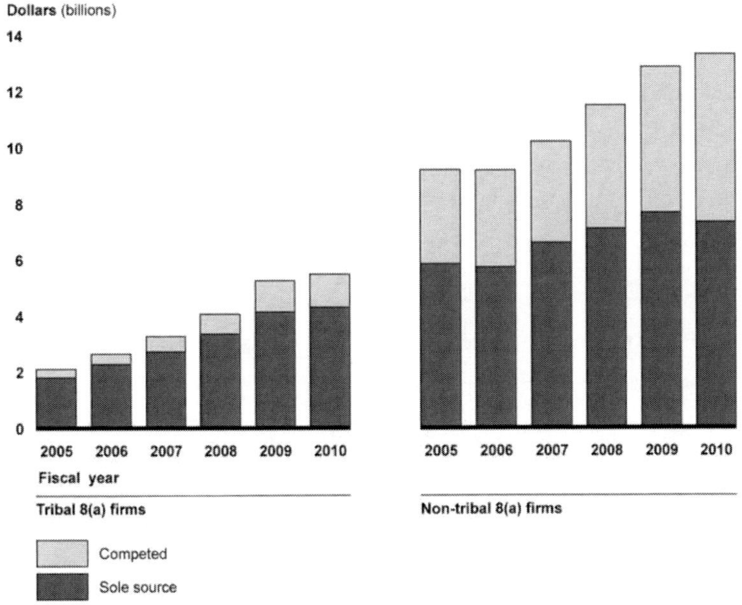

Source: GAO analysis based on information from FPDS-NG.
Note: Obligation amounts are inflation adjusted to 2010 dollars.

Figure 4. Competitive and Sole-Source Obligations to Tribal and Non-Tribal 8(a) Firms, Fiscal Years 2005 through 2010 (in billions).

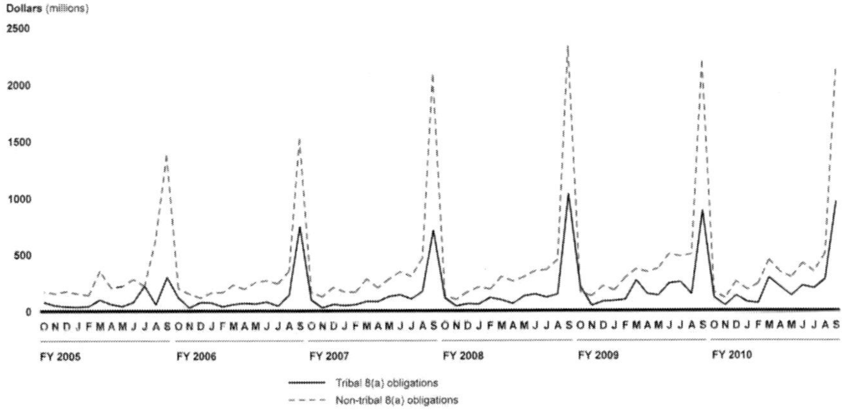

Source: GAO analysis based on information from FPDS-NG.
Note: Obligation amounts are inflation adjusted to 2010 dollars.

Figure 5. Monthly Sole-Source Obligations for New Awards to Tribal and Non-Tribal 8(a) Firms, Fiscal Year 2005 through 2010.

One tribal 8(a) firm's business plan we reviewed, submitted to SBA, alluded to increased obligations at the end of the fiscal year and noted that it changes its marketing strategy accordingly during that time. The plan noted that "[Our] business is not seasonal with the exception of the end of fiscal year spending for the U.S. Government. During this period, we concentrate our efforts directly at the government by increasing our visits and solicitations at the locations where we have the most successful and loyal contacts."

Sole-Source Contracts to Tribal 8(a) Firms Viewed as Expedient, but Could Lead to Missed Opportunities for Savings

Contracting officials at the agencies we reviewed, similar to what we reported in 2006, told us that using tribal firms under the 8(a) program allows them to award sole-source contracts for any value quickly, easily and legally.[14] They further stated these awards help procuring agencies to meet their small business goals, but added that the program offices' preference for using the same firms for follow-on contracts also plays a role.[15] Our review of 79 sole-source tribal 8(a) contracts revealed some of the methods used by contracting officials to determine price reasonableness in a sole-source environment. However in several cases we found that contracting officers were moving away from sole-source tribal 8(a) contracts toward competition. We also found examples where tribal 8(a) contracts that had previously been awarded on a sole-source basis were competed, resulting in savings.

Tribal 8(a) Sole-Source Contracts Viewed as Quick and Easy and Contributing to Small Business Goals

Contracting officials viewed sole-source contract awards to tribal 8(a) firms as a way to expedite the federal acquisition process, avoid some potential bid protests, and help them meet their agencies' small business goals. Prior to SBA's acceptance of any sole-source requirement into the 8(a) program, the procuring agency need only identify a qualified 8(a) firm and obtain approval from SBA to award a contract. It is the procuring agency's responsibility to conduct market research, including determining whether offers can be obtained from two or more firms at fair market prices. However,

SBA also considers market research requirements to be satisfied when a participant in the 8(a) program self-markets its abilities to a procuring agency and is subsequently offered a sole-source 8(a) requirement.[16]

Award of Sole-Source Tribal 8(a) Contracts Allows Expedited Acquisition Planning and Market Research

Acquisition planning activities are intended to ensure that the government meets its needs in the most effective, economical, and timely manner possible. Some contracting officers awarded sole-source 8(a) contracts to tribal firms because this approach allowed them to avoid lengthy acquisition planning and market research procedures, thereby expediting the procurement process.[17] For example, documentation in a Department of Homeland Security contract revealed that the contracting official awarded a $96 million sole-source contract to a tribal 8(a) firm because this was the most streamlined approach to obtain services. According to the contract file, the agency saved considerable time in the acquisition process and thereby ensured a timely award. In another example, one contracting officer told us that she sees many more sole-source contracts to tribal 8(a) firms at the end of the fiscal year, likely because of poor acquisition planning. Recalling a time when a program office needed to award a contract quickly during the fourth quarter of the fiscal year, she said she was able to award the contract on a sole-source basis to a tribal 8(a) firm within 2 weeks. She estimated that to award the contract competitively would have taken 60 to 90 days.

In another scenario, DOD contracting officials used the expedited procurement process of sole-source contracts to tribal 8(a) firms to maintain the quality of critical services. They awarded two contracts— each valued at over $500 million for a 10-year period (base period plus 9 option years)—for base engineering support at two different military installations. A large part of the justification for this acquisition strategy was that annual DOD appropriations acts permitted the department to avoid using the Office of Management and Budget's *Circular No. A-76* competitive sourcing process by contracting with tribal 8(a) firms.[18] The purpose of the competitive sourcing process is to determine whether the government should be performing a function with its personnel or contracting those functions to private sector firms. DOD officials believed awarding the sole-source contracts was necessary, since concerns about the time frames to conduct the A-76 process—which officials at one base estimated could take up to 3 years—were causing the government employees performing the work to become increasingly concerned about their job security and to seek employment elsewhere.

In some cases, as allowed, contracting officials awarded sole-source contracts to tribal 8(a) firms even though market research had revealed other firms capable of performing the work. For example, Army contracting officials' request for information for medical services resulted in six firms' submitting comments. However, citing the current contract's expiration time frame, the contracting officer stated that a successful competition would require a great deal of acquisition planning and, as such, would likely result in a break in services. In another example, market research identified 93 potential contractors for a base engineering support requirement; several of which were known to possess the capabilities to handle the requirement if it were competitively solicited. In fact, the previous contract for this requirement had been competitively awarded in the 8(a) program, with seven offers received. Our review of the acquisition plan and discussion with the contracting officer revealed that the reason for awarding the sole-source follow-on contract was because of the significant delay in obtaining the statement of work from the program office. Because the requirement was critical and the new contractor would have to "hit the ground running," a sole-source contract was awarded to a tribal 8(a) firm that had subcontracted with the incumbent contractor.

At one Army Corps of Engineers location we visited, contracting officials told us that they put basic ordering agreements (BOA) in place—such as the one we reviewed for design and construction services with a tribal 8(a) firm—because BOAs can be quickly set up, sometimes in only a matter of hours. The regulations require that an agency offer, and SBA accept, each order under a BOA to the 8(a) program prior to award, because the BOA itself is not a contract.[19] As part of this process, SBA would ensure that the tribal 8(a) firm still meets the size standard for the NAICS code for the requirement at the time the order is offered to SBA. However, we found that the contracting officer was not offering each order under this $10 million BOA (which had been awarded in June 2009) to SBA, in violation of FAR and SBA regulations. The DOD contracting official in this case sent notices of the orders to the SBA district office after the award. SBA district officials did not follow up to determine why these orders had not been offered prior to the award. By not offering each order under the BOA, there is a risk that a tribal 8(a) firm could outgrow the size standard and be improperly awarded a sole-source contract through the 8(a) program. In subsequent discussions, SBA and an Army Corps of Engineers legal representative confirmed that all orders under BOAs in the 8(a) program should be offered to SBA. According to the legal representative, the contracting office is no longer using BOAs to meet its requirements and is instead using indefinite quantity contracts.[20]

Reduced Likelihood That Tribal 8(a) Sole-Source Contracts Will Be Protested

Tribal 8(a) sole-source contracts are also attractive because there are limitations on their ability to be protested. Although 8(a) sole-source awards have been protested, the following issues may not be challenged of any 8(a) participant by any party, either to SBA or any administrative forum as part of a bid or other contract protest: (1) the eligibility of the participant for a sole-source or competitive 8(a) requirement, (2) the NAICS code assigned to a sole-source 8(a) requirement, or (3) the size status of a nominated participant for a sole-source 8(a) procurement.[21] According to contracting officials, bid protests can result in significant and costly delays and potentially disrupt critical services. Moreover, the officials stated that responding to bid protests absorbs their already limited time and resources. One tribal 8(a) company, in its marketing materials to the government, mentioned that one of the many benefits of a sole-source award to their company was that it would not be subject to a bid protest.

Competitive 8(a) awards can be protested by other 8(a) firms, and we found an example of this in one of the seven competitively awarded contracts we reviewed. After an 8(a) contract was awarded competitively to a tribal firm, the incumbent firm's sister subsidiary, who had competed under the solicitation, protested the award.[22] This sister subsidiary did not receive the award because its proposal relied on the past performance of its sister firm (the incumbent). According to the solicitation's instructions, past performance of sister firms would not be considered as highly as the firm's own past performance.[23] Further, its offer was 86 percent higher than that of the winning tribal 8(a) contractor. As a result of the protest, the expiring contract was extended 5 months, resulting in over $800,000 in additional revenue for the incumbent firm.

Sole-Source Tribal 8(a) Contracts Can Help Agencies Meet Small Business Goals

Another reason contracting officials gave for awarding sole source tribal 8(a) contracts is to help their agencies meet their small business prime contracting goals. Some tribal 8(a) firms also recognize that this is an attractive feature and promote it in their marketing materials. However, at one location we visited, agency officials told us that they chose to compete a follow-on procurement outside of the 8(a) program even though they knew it would significantly affect their ability to meet their small business goals. The previous 8(a) contractor had been awarded a 5-year, $250 million dollar contract. Obligations under this contract had helped the agency meet its small business goals. Nevertheless, agency officials, including the small business advocate, thought the potential to obtain a better price and service through full and open competition was more important at that time.

Officials Also Award Sole- Source Contracts to Tribal 8(a) Firms for Continuity

Contracting officials we spoke with noted that some program officials prefer to continue working with specific tribal 8(a) firms, especially when program officials had established a working rapport with the incumbent contractors. Our prior work has shown that program officials generally have a preference for working with incumbent firms.[24] Program officials play an important role in the contracting process—developing requirements, performing market research, and interfacing with contractors. For one Army contract we reviewed to provide direct healthcare services at military medical-treatment facilities, program officials had decided that a follow-on sole-source 8(a) contract award to one of the incumbent firm's sister subsidiaries was the best option because there was a potential for risk if the procurement start date was not met. Additionally, in its proposal, the incumbent's sister subsidiary highlighted the fact that SBA regulations permitted it to share senior management with the incumbent and that as a result, their services were provided under the same team.

We found instances in which contracting officials awarded bridge or follow-on sole-source contracts to incumbent tribal 8(a) firms or to their sister subsidiaries for continuity.[25]

- Forest Service contracting officials had a history of awarding sole-source bridge or follow-on contracts for similar requirements to the same incumbent 8(a) firm or one of its sister subsidiaries. The contracting official responsible for the three contracts in our sample explained that the program office pressured her to continue awarding to this particular firm because the program office believed that awarding the requirement to a new contractor would cause a disruption in services. One of these contracts—a $125-million sole-source 8(a) contract for computer hardware and enterprise software—was awarded to a firm's sister subsidiary when the incumbent was no longer eligible to receive 8(a) contracts. An email from an official from the sister firm to the contracting officer, in suggesting that the new contract be awarded to the sister firm, told the agency that all incumbent personnel working on the contract, as well as equipment, would be transferred over and that essentially the agency "will see only a name change in the firm providing the service."

- A contracting official at the Department of Energy told us that she awarded a sole-source contract for facility maintenance and support services to the sister subsidiary of a tribal 8(a) firm because the incumbent firm had graduated from the 8(a) program, thus making it ineligible for the follow-on contract. Further, she stated that this made the transition very easy to manage, since nearly 100 percent of the incumbent's staff transferred directly to the sister firm.

We also found examples where bridge contracts to tribal 8(a) firms were used to ensure continuity while competing the follow-on requirement; however, it was not always a smooth transition. In one case, a contracting officer at an Army acquisition activity awarded a one-year bridge contract to the incumbent tribal 8(a) firm to avoid unnecessary delays and provide sufficient time to compete the requirement in the future. The incumbent's contract—awarded out of a different Army contracting office—had been terminated after one and a half years on the grounds that it was legally insufficient. However, when awarding the bridge contract, contracting officials learned that the incumbent contractor's employees had assisted the Army in developing the follow-on requirement. The contracting officer had the contractor put in place a plan to mitigate this conflict of interest, but still awarded the sole-source bridge contract to meet the immediate need. In another case, Army officials tried to award a task order under an existing contract as a bridge contract to maintain the service while they competed the follow-on award. According to Army officials, the tribal 8(a) firm refused to negotiate, stating it would only agree to a 6-month bridge contract with three 1-year option periods. The contracting officer told us that they believed they were in a bind, agreed to the terms, and ended up exercising all 3 option years. The follow-on requirement is currently being competed.

Potential Impact of New Sole- Source Justification Requirement Unclear

In March 2011, the FAR was revised to incorporate a new rule, pursuant to section 811 of the National Defense Authorization Act for Fiscal Year 2010, which requires a written justification for sole-source 8(a) contracts over $20 million. The justification must be approved by the appropriate officials—dictated by dollar thresholds—and be publicly posted within 14 days of award. This provision may have an impact on how quickly and easily sole-source tribal 8(a) contracts are awarded. The new justification must include, at a minimum

- a description of the needs of the agency that will be addressed by the contract,
- specification of the statutory provision allowing for the exception to competition,
- a determination that the use of a sole-source contract is in the best interest of the agency concerned,
- a determination that the anticipated cost of the contract will be fair and reasonable, and
- other matters the head of the agency would like included.

While these requirements were not in effect for the contracts we reviewed, we discussed with the contracting officials the potential impact on future sole-source tribal 8(a) awards. Their opinions varied. Several officials stated that it will be more difficult to award sole-source contracts to tribal 8(a) firms, and in some cases these officials said they were pleased to have a tool to encourage program offices to increase competition. Others thought it would make no difference, stating that the justification is simply additional paperwork for the contract file. Still others stated that the new requirement will not affect them because their office had already moved away from awarding sole-source 8(a) contracts to tribally owned firms toward more competition. Some officials attributed this change in attitude in part to congressional and media attention on large dollar, sole-source awards to tribally owned firms.

Various Methods Used to Negotiate Prices for Sole-Source Awards, and Some Savings Realized through Subsequent Competition

When awarding an 8(a) contract, contracting officers are required to determine that the overall price is a fair market price, which can be done through a cost or price analysis. The fair market price does not have to be the lowest price. However in a sole-source environment, there are increased concerns that the prices may not be the best for the government, as competition is the cornerstone of the acquisition system and a critical tool for achieving the best possible return on investment for taxpayers. These concerns would be no different under non-tribal 8(a) sole-source contracts. We found that contracting officials used various methods to determine price reasonableness of contractors' proposed costs or prices. We also found examples where the follow-on requirements were subsequently competed and agency officials estimated savings.

In finding a fair market price, contracting officers must first determine that the costs or prices proposed are fair and reasonable. According to the FAR, price analysis shall be used when certified cost or pricing data are not required. Price analysis is the process of examining and evaluating a proposed price without evaluating its separate cost elements and proposed profit. One of the preferred price analysis techniques is comparing proposed prices from more than one contractor in response to a competitive solicitation, as adequate price competition establishes a fair and reasonable price. The other preferred price analysis method is a comparison to historical pricing for the same or similar items. When using this method, however, the contracting officer must ensure that the pricing is a valid basis for comparison, such as ensuring that significant time has not lapsed between the prior acquisition and the present one. In addition, the prior price must be adjusted to account for materially differing terms and conditions, quantities, and market and economic factors. If contracting officers determine that these two techniques are unavailable or insufficient, they are encouraged to use other methods appropriate to the circumstances, such as comparison with competitive published price lists or independent government estimates. The FAR also states that cost analysis shall be used to evaluate the reasonableness of individual cost elements when certified cost or pricing data are required (however, price analysis is used to determine that the overall price offered is fair and reasonable). Cost analysis is the review and evaluation of any separate cost elements and profit or fee in an offeror's or contractor's proposal. Some cost analysis techniques include evaluating the government's need for proposed cost elements, verifying labor rates, or comparing proposed costs to actual costs previously incurred by the same offeror. Cost analysis may also be used to determine cost reasonableness or cost realism when a fair and reasonable price cannot be determined through price analysis alone.

Comparison to Historical Pricing or Published Price Lists

For many of the sole-source contracts in our review, agency officials compared contractors' proposed prices to the prices on the prior contract, U.S.

General Services Administration (GSA) schedule prices, or pricing data from other sources. The following cases indicate the complexities of this price analysis technique. For example:

- A price analyst at the Social Security Administration found that a tribal 8(a) firm's proposed prices for a $100-million sole-source contract were generally 5 to 192 percent higher than the prior, non-8(a) contractor's prices. As a result, the price analyst recommended negotiating price reductions with the tribal firm. The contracting officer then performed an additional analysis of the same proposal and noted that the tribal firm's proposed rates were 8 to 51 percent *lower* than the prior firm's GSA schedule rates and were at or below the schedule rates of a subcontractor. The documented analysis noted that comparing the proposed rates to the incumbent contractor's rates could be potentially misleading because performance problems also needed to be taken into account and that the incumbent contractor had not always provided qualified personnel, among other things. The tribal 8(a) firm's proposed prices were accepted.
- For another Social Security Administration contract, the contracting officer evaluated the tribal 8(a) firm's proposed prices for a sole-source, fixed-price contract based on pricing information from the current contract and noticed a significant increase in the tribal 8(a) firm's price for installation and storage of the equipment being purchased. Upon further investigation, the contracting officer learned that the previous pricing had not accounted for substantial government delays that had added to the costs; the new proposal was attempting to appropriately include those costs. The contracting officer noted that the government would work to improve the inefficiencies that were causing this increase in cost, and based on these circumstances, the proposed higher price was determined fair and reasonable.

Independent Government Cost Estimates Are Another Tool to Assess Price Reasonableness

Independent government cost estimates were also used to determine price reasonableness for the sole-source contracts in our review. The examples below illustrate some challenges faced when the estimates relied in part on outdated costs or inaccurate assumptions. For example:

- In one Army contract, the initial independent government estimate had to be revised from about $49 million to about $100 million, because it had not taken into account many different factors, such as travel and overtime for subcontractors. The contract was awarded for about $113 million.
- In another example at the Army, an independent government estimate was $2.7 million, compared to the contractor's proposal of $4.7 million. The price negotiation memorandum noted that the government's estimate was found to have several missing items, outdated estimates, and inaccurate assumptions. The estimate was used as the primary basis for conducting negotiations with the contractor and to determine that the contractor's higher price was fair and reasonable. The contract was ultimately awarded for about $4.0 million.

For one Army contract we reviewed, the contracting officer told us that she stopped using a competed, single-award indefinite quantity contract to a tribal 8(a) firm because the firm's proposals for two of three task orders were significantly over the government estimates and the government officials did not believe they were getting a fair market price. In this case, the Army had simultaneously competed and awarded the base contract and the first task order. The contractor's proposed price for the second task order, however, was almost $6 million, whereas the initial government estimate was just below $4 million. Contracting and program officials pushed back on the contractor's proposed price, but the firm would not negotiate. The government ultimately awarded the second task order at the contractor's proposed price. The contracting officer told us that the same thing happened on the third task order, so the Army officials canceled the procurement and stopped using that contract.

Some officials told us that developing independent government estimates can be challenging, as the pricing environment can change and the estimate—which may be prepared 6 months to a year prior to contract award—can become outdated before negotiations begin. For example, when construction work is in high demand, prices for those services can increase over the course of a year, according to contracting officers. Other contracting officials told us that they question how independent the government estimates are when the tribal 8(a) incumbent works closely with the program staff who develop the estimates.

Contracting Officers May Use Audits to Negotiate Lower Overall Prices

For many of the sole-source awards we reviewed, contracting officials requested support from the Defense Contract Audit Agency (DCAA) to evaluate the reasonableness of the proposed costs.[26] Some contracting officials effectively used this support to negotiate a lower overall price. For example, in our review of one DOD contract, DCAA submitted findings to the procuring agency 3 months prior to the award date, citing, among other things, $6.9 million in unsupported costs. Consequently, the contracting officials negotiated a 15 percent reduction of the proposed price, which amounted to a savings of nearly $9 million. In an Army contract, contracting officials agreed with the lower rates suggested by DCAA for certain cost categories and ultimately negotiated those rates with the tribal 8(a) firm, reducing the contract price by over $6 million.

In another instance, agency officials awarded a sole-source contract to a tribal 8(a) firm quickly to ensure that critical services were maintained, but asked DCAA to audit the proposal with the understanding that the officials would further negotiate the costs after award based on the findings. DCAA's assessment of the firm's proposed costs was provided 2 months after the contract's award. The audit questioned some of the contractor's proposed costs, such as duplicative labor positions and staff positions that were vacant but for which salaries, wages, fringes, and retirement contributions were included in the final cost of the contract. The contracting officers faced challenges negotiating the contract's price, as they were still negotiating some of these costs with the contractor nearly a year and a half after contract award.

Some Contracting Officers Used Alpha Negotiation Procedures

For sole source procurements, the government and contractor may use what is known as "alpha" procedures, where they work as a team during negotiations to define or refine requirements and come to agreement on prices. A number of contracting officers had used this method to work with a tribal 8(a) contractor to agree on a fair market price. One contracting official told us that negotiating prices face-to-face with the contractor using alpha procedures is easier and less time intensive, primarily because he can tell the 8(a) contractor how much funding he has to spend. From there, the contractor can explain to him what the government needs to "take off the table" and what items in the scope of work the contractor can provide at that price. Another contracting official told us that he used alpha procedures because the program office had failed to set all of the contract requirements prior to commencing negotiations with the tribal 8(a) contractor.

Contracting officials at one location we visited noted that alpha contracting in a sole-source environment can lead to the best deal for the government for a variety of reasons, such as leveraging the insight of technical experts throughout the price negotiation process and providing a forum for the contractor to ask for additional clarification about the government's requirements. At another location we visited, one contracting official told us that he believed the government got a better price using alpha procedures than by using full and open competition when contracting for construction of identical buildings. He attributed this in part to the fact that the contractor in the alpha process had a better understanding of the government requirements and the government did not have to go back and correct or make adjustments to the contract.

With Focus on Competition, Some Estimate That Savings Occurred

Several contracting officers we spoke with noted that they are moving away from sole-source contracts to tribal 8(a) firms and towards competition. We recently highlighted the benefits of competition in federal government contracting, including that it can save money, improve contractor performance, and promote accountability for results.[27] We recommended appropriate actions, including that both program and contracting officials encourage competition, so that federal agencies would have greater opportunities to take advantage of the effectiveness of the marketplace and potentially achieve billions of dollars in cost savings. Recent policy and guidance from agencies, most significantly the Office of Management and Budget (OMB) and DOD, have also emphasized the importance of competition.[28] With regard to ANCs, the Acting Deputy Assistant Secretary of the Army (Procurement) issued a memo in January 2011, stating that high-dollar sole-source awards to 8(a) ANC firms should be the exception rather than the rule, and laid out the expectation that these awards be scrutinized to ensure they are in the government's best interest. Further, in November 2011, DOD's Director of Defense Procurement and Acquisition Policy called for a review of all active sole-source contracts to ANCs that were awarded prior to the new requirement for a written justification for awards over $20 million. As part of the review, DOD services, agencies, and activities must review the justifications (if any) that support the contract awards and describe actions to ensure there is no abuse of these types of contracts.

In the sole-source contracts we reviewed, we found examples where the follow-on requirements were subsequently competed, resulting in savings according to agency officials.

- The Air Force awarded a contract competitively for base operation support and, according to officials, saved about $17 million for a requirement that was valued at over $100 million. Officials stated that the previous contractor had high management costs.
- At the Army, we reviewed an approximately $8.9 million sole-source contract with a tribal 8(a) firm for one year of medical services. The contracting activity recompeted the follow-on requirement, and the contracting officer estimated savings of $2.3 million annually, for a total of $11.5 million over the life of the contract.
- At the Federal Emergency Management Agency, the contracting officer told us that when the follow-on to the sole-source tribal 8(a) contract in our review had been competed among small businesses, the labor rates on the new contract were, with one exception, between 5 and 46 percent lower than the previous sole-source contract.
- Department of Energy officials told us that they competed a requirement that was previously awarded sole source to a tribal 8(a) firm, and while they could not estimate dollar savings, they believed they were getting better performance as a result of the competition.

AGENCY OVERSIGHT OF SUBCONTRACTING UNDER TRIBAL 8(A) CONTRACTS CONTINUES TO BE LACKING

To ensure that 8(a) firms do not pass along the benefits of their contracts to their subcontractors, regulations limit the amount of work that can be performed by subcontractors. Specifically, for service contracts with subcontracting activity, the 8(a) firm must incur at least 50 percent of the personnel costs with its own employees (for general construction contracts, the firm must incur at least 15 percent of the personnel costs).[29] In 2006, we reported that procuring agency contracting officers were not monitoring compliance with the limitations on the percentage of work performed by subcontractors as required—largely because they were confused about whose responsibility it was to do so.[30] Based on our recommendations, SBA took some actions to clarify this issue, including providing training to contracting officers and revising its partnership agreements with procuring agencies. Nevertheless, we have continued to find that monitoring of subcontracting limitations is not routinely occurring due to a lack of clarity as to who is responsible for the monitoring and uncertainty on the part of contracting officers about how to conduct the monitoring. Of the 87 contracts in our review, 71 had one or more subcontractors. We found no evidence of regular and systematic monitoring of the limitations on subcontracting.[31] Some of these contracts had large dollar values, up to $500 million. When the subcontracting limitations are not being monitored, there is an increased risk that an inappropriate degree of the work is being done by large business subcontractors rather than the 8(a) firm. These risks can be significant given the large dollar value contracts awarded to tribal 8(a) firms.

Confusion Remains about Accountability for Monitoring Subcontracting Limitations

In response to our 2006 recommendations, SBA clarified in its partnership agreements with the procuring agencies that it is the contracting officer's responsibility to monitor compliance with the limits on subcontracting under 8(a) contracts.[32] In addition, SBA standardized language in its 8(a) acceptance letters to state that contracting officers are responsible for the monitoring.[33] SBA also provided additional training and guidance for agency contracting officers about this responsibility, among other 8(a) contracting requirements. Even with these actions, however, we still found that some contracting officers do not understand that ensuring compliance with the limitations on subcontracting is their responsibility. Some stated that it was SBA's responsibility as part of the annual review process for tribal 8(a) firms, and officials for one agency thought that it was ultimately the prime contractor's responsibility.[34] A contracting official from the State Department told us that he did not have the time or staff to monitor compliance, but he believed that the prime contractor self- monitored because the firm was hiring some subcontractor employees to work for it to ensure that the required work percentages were met.

We found situations where there is an increased risk that the subcontractor may be performing more than the limitations allow. In some cases, these subcontractors were large firms or firms that had graduated from the 8(a) program, yet the government was not monitoring compliance with the limits on subcontracting. For example, in one case, the subcontractor to a tribal 8(a) firm under a base engineering support contract had held the prior contract for the requirement, and the subcontractor's president had part-ownership in the tribal 8(a) firm. For another contract, to build an airplane hangar at an Air Force base—in which the percentage of work subcontracted was not monitored—the tribal 8(a) firm had subcontracted with a large business that had extensive experience in hangar building. During the negotiation process, after much discussion about the project, a government representative asked the tribal 8(a) firm what work it would be doing; up to that point the subcontractor had been answering all the questions. In another example, for construction of an aircraft facility at another Air Force base, the prime contractor stated in its proposal that it could not meet the 15 percent of work requirement, and thus a legal review initially found the pending award to be legally insufficient and unacceptable. The contracting specialist wrote a note on the legal memo stating that the prime contractor would meet the required work percentages, with no additional explanation. Notwithstanding the concerns raised, the contract was awarded. The contracting officer told us that she does not monitor the percentage of work that is subcontracted on this contract.

Although contracting officers should consider all applicable regulations when awarding and administering 8(a) contracts, several contracting officers we spoke with told us they depend primarily on the requirements outlined in the FAR for guidance. The FAR only directs contracting officers to include the "limitations on subcontracting" clause—under which the prime contractor agrees to perform a certain percentage of the contract work itself in its 8(a) contract. The FAR does not state who is accountable for monitoring compliance with the required percentages. While the partnership agreements between SBA and the agencies clearly state that the procuring agencies are responsible for the monitoring, these agreements are signed by high level SBA and agency procurement officials; contracting officials may not be aware of the content of the agreements.

Adding to the confusion over which agency is responsible for monitoring subcontracting, in reviewing 8(a) files in the SBA Alaska district office, we found examples where prime contractors had reported to SBA that they were complying with the limitations on subcontracting. However, SBA officials told us that they do not consistently collect this information from 8(a) firms and that it is ultimately the responsibility of the procuring agency to monitor compliance.

Contracting Officers Unclear about How to Monitor Subcontracting Limitations

Many contracting officials told us they do not know how to monitor the percentage of work that is subcontracted. Based on our review of agency contract files, data were not readily available, making it difficult to determine how much work was being performed by the prime contractor versus the subcontractor. For example, contractor invoices in some of the files we reviewed did not reflect the subcontracting activity. And for those invoices that did include subcontractor information, the separation between labor and materials costs was unclear. This information would be needed for contracting officers to properly monitor compliance with the limits on subcontracting, which excludes the costs of materials. Some contracting officials noted that the prime contractor itself would have ready access to the subcontracting percentages (such as in its financial systems). One contracting official noted that contractor invoices for time- and-materials services under a contract in our sample identified the subcontracted work, but the invoices for fixed-price services, billed under the same contract, did not. She estimated that it would take her several weeks to calculate the percentage of work that was subcontracted.

A further complication pertains to monitoring subcontracting under indefinite quantity contracts, the government's use of which is now outpacing stand-alone contracts. Of the 41 indefinite quantity contracts in our sample that had subcontractors, we found no evidence that the subcontracting limits were being routinely monitored. SBA regulations state that the 8(a) participant must demonstrate semi-annually whether it has incurred 50 percent of personnel costs with its own employees for the combined total of all task or delivery orders at the end of each 6-month period.[35] However, the FAR does not cross-reference to this provision or otherwise describe how to monitor subcontract limitations in indefinite quantity contracts.

Contracting officials told us they would appreciate additional guidance regarding methods they should employ to track compliance with the limits on subcontracting. The FAR is silent on this subject, and the SBA 8(a) regulation does not provide detailed instructions on how to do so. In the absence of specific guidance, some of the contracting officers we spoke with pointed to techniques that they have used to try to gauge the amount of work that is subcontracted. For example, one official said that he monitored subcontractors by "walking the ground," so he can easily sight- check contractor badges to determine who is a prime contractor and who is a subcontractor. In another scenario, officials stated that they visit the worksite to check the company names on the trucks parked there. Others relied on their personal knowledge of the contractors, stating that because they were very familiar with the prime contractor, they would know if the firm was not performing its required percentage of the work. And still others tallied the number of workers employed by the prime versus subcontractor to get a general picture of the amount subcontracted, but did not calculate the percentage of labor costs associated with the subcontractors. While these actions are ways to get a general sense of subcontracting activity, they are not adequate to determine the extent of personnel costs that are incurred by the contractor.

Many contracting officials also told us they reviewed contractor proposals to verify that the prime contractor planned to perform the required percentage of the work. However, this level of review alone does not ensure compliance with the limitations on subcontracting clause because subcontractors, and the amount of work they do, can change once the contract is awarded. In addition, contracting officers may not even be aware that work is being subcontracted. The tribal 8(a) contractor's proposal for one contract we reviewed, for example, noted as a benefit to the government that the contractor's own employees would be indistinguishable from those of its subcontractor. We also found cases in our review where contracting officials inadvertently learned that their prime contractors were using subcontractors. One Department of Agriculture official told us that he did not realize certain positions were going to be subcontracted until he questioned a particular wage rate during the negotiation process, and the firm stated that it needed to seek additional information from the subcontractor. In another instance, a contracting official at the Department of Justice was unaware that the prime contractor had subcontracted work until we brought it to her attention based on our review of the contract file. She added that often "the contracting officer is the last to know" about the prime contractor's hiring subcontractors, because of a lack of communication among the contractor, program office, and contracting office. In yet another example, a DOD contracting officer said that he only learned that work was being subcontracted when a subcontractor employee was caught speeding on the base.

During our review of contract files, we found a few instances where the file included a recently performed analysis of subcontracting percentages that appeared to have been prepared in anticipation of our visit. In one case, at the Centers for Medicare and Medicaid Services, an analysis, which the contracting officer said was prepared for our visit, showed that the prime contractor had subcontracted almost 72 percent of the total costs for the 3-

month base period of a 5-year, almost $205 million contract, but a few years into the contract the overall subcontracting level had dropped to about 40 percent. The contracting officer explained that he knew that the 8(a) firm would have to initially subcontract out a substantial portion of the work, but the expectation was that the contractor would meet the required work percentage over the course of the period of performance. In another case, a recent analysis of the subcontracting percentages for several 6-month periods on an Army indefinite quantity contract showed that the prime contractor was performing the required percentage of the work, but when we asked the contracting officer about the analysis, he was not sure who had completed it or the basis for the figures. In another example, a document in a Food and Drug Administration contract file showed the prime contractor was performing the required percentage of the work. The contracting officer said that, in preparation for our visit, she had requested the analysis from the contractor, as she did not have the information to do it herself. She told us that she requests this information periodically from the vendor; however, there was no record of these periodic analyses in the contract file. We also talked to contracting officials who told us that they requested regular reports from the contractor on the amount of work subcontracted, but when we asked for examples of the reports, none could be provided, and there were no examples of these reports in the contract files.

SBA's New Regulations Will be Difficult to Implement, and Other Problems and Practices Have Not Been Addressed

SBA made the first significant revision to 8(a) program regulations, effective March 14, 2011, in over 10 years, aimed at clarifying program rules, correcting misinterpretations, and addressing program issues. The revised rules include new requirements that will affect tribal firm participation in the 8(a) program, such as rules related to sole-source follow-on contracts and work performed by joint ventures. However, SBA will have difficulty enforcing some of these new regulations given the information currently available. Further, SBA, in its regulations or elsewhere, has still not addressed some issues we raised in our 2006 report. Finally, in this review we discuss practices that highlight how some tribal 8(a) firms operate, in effect, like large businesses due to their parent corporation's backing and relationships with their sister subsidiaries. SBA has not reviewed these practices to determine whether they are acceptable given the business development purpose of the 8(a) program.

SBA Lacks Data to Implement and Enforce Some of the New Regulations

Although the recent SBA rule changes are intended, in part, to address tribally owned firms' participation in the 8(a) program, SBA does not have critical data it needs to implement or enforce compliance with some of the new requirements. These include new restrictions on agencies' ability to award sole-source follow-on contracts to firms under the same tribal entity and restrictions on work performed by the non-8(a) partner in a joint venture. SBA headquarters officials told us they are currently in the initial stages of developing the requirements for a new system intended to provide necessary data on 8(a) firms, and estimate that it will be operational between September 2012 and January 2013. They are also in the process of re-writing their Standard Operating Procedures for district officials to implement the new regulations; however, they could not estimate at this time when the final version will be completed.

SBA Will Have Difficulty Tracking Sole-Source Follow-on Contracts with Sister Subsidiaries

In 2006, we reported that ANC 8(a) firms were taking advantage of their ability to create new subsidiaries to win follow-on work from subsidiaries that had left the 8(a) program. One of the new SBA rules prohibits the award of successive follow-on sole-source 8(a) contracts to multiple firms owned by the same tribal entity. Specifically, agencies are now prohibited from awarding a follow-on 8(a) sole-source contract to another subsidiary firm owned by the same entity—also called a sister subsidiary.[36] In its explanation of this new provision, SBA stated that having one subsidiary take over work previously performed by a sister subsidiary does not advance the business development of two distinct firms. SBA expects that, when it accepts multiple firms under the same tribal entity into the 8(a) program, each firm will operate and grow independently in line with the business development purposes of the program. SBA's intention was to address a negative perception that businesses could operate in the 8(a) program in perpetuity by changing their structure or form to continue to perform work as they had under previous contracts. As an example of this perception, we found that one tribal 8(a) firm stated in its marketing materials that it would "never graduate" from the 8(a) program. Agency officials told us that it is their general impression that by awarding follow-on contracts to the incumbent firm's sister subsidiary, they are, for all intents and purposes, working with the same company.

In our current review, we found multiple examples of follow-on sole-source 8(a) contracts being awarded to a sister subsidiary. While these contracts had all been awarded prior to the effective date of the new rule, these examples suggest that it is not unusual for agencies to turn to sister subsidiaries for follow-on sole-source 8(a) contracts. For example:

- When we spoke to one contracting officer's representative with the Army in May 2011, we found that he was unaware of the new regulation. He explained that when a tribal firm graduates from the 8(a) program, his office would typically award a sole-source follow-on contract to one of the firm's sister subsidiaries based upon the past performance of the incumbent. Noting that a current sole-source tribal 8(a) contract to provide research and development support was set to expire in 2012 and that the incumbent was graduating from the 8(a) program, he stated that it made sense to award the follow-on to one of the firm's sister subsidiaries, especially since the incumbent had performed well. After we told him this was no longer permissible under SBA regulations, he said that the new rule put a "kink" in his plans and that he would need to start planning right away to ensure there was adequate time to successfully award the requirement competitively.

In another example from our review, a procuring agency had awarded a follow-on contract to a sister subsidiary without realizing the relationship between the firms. In September 2007, the Social Security Administration awarded a $48 million 8(a) sole- source follow-on contract for information technology support services. The incumbent 8(a) ANC firm recommended that the agency make the award to its protégé, as the incumbent was no longer in the 8(a) program. When we spoke to agency officials in July 2011, the agency was not aware that the protégé firm, which received the follow-on award, was also a sister subsidiary of the incumbent. According to the officials, they will rely on SBA to know if a firm targeted for a follow- on procurement is eligible for an 8(a) award based on the new rules.

Although prohibiting this practice of awarding sole-source follow-on contracts to sister subsidiaries of 8(a) firms is a positive step toward curbing some perceived abuses of the 8(a) program, the required information is not always available to enforce this new rule. For example, SBA's data system for tracking 8(a) participants does not provide district offices with the full information needed to track compliance. District officials have access only to information on the firms that they service. Yet a number of tribal entities have firms in multiple locations throughout the country, and those firms are serviced by different SBA district offices. To illustrate, one ANC parent company has eight subsidiaries serviced in six different district offices. Because SBA's Alaska district office services the majority of ANC 8(a) firms, its insight into the activities of those parent corporations' subsidiaries may be greater than that of other SBA districts, which may service only one of several subsidiaries under the same parent corporation. When we visited the Alaska district office 7 weeks after the new rule had taken effect, we found evidence that SBA had turned down a follow-on contract offer from a procuring agency because the contract violated the new regulation; district officials informed us that they had declined four to five other contract offers for the same reason. However, the officials explained that they maintain paper files and that they would have limited procurement history information—including information about the prior, incumbent firm—unless the requirement had always been serviced by that district. Conversely, officials at an SBA district office that services relatively few tribal 8(a) firms told us that they have not turned down any offer letters that violate this new regulation, but that they also would not necessarily know if the incumbent was a sister firm given the information they can access in the 8(a) tracking system.

SBA headquarters officials are aware of the limitations of the data system and told us that they are currently developing a new system that is intended to provide a more global view of tribal entities to the officials at all district offices. They are also considering ways to access more information on a contract's procurement history, including linking their new system to FPDS-NG to obtain more information on 8(a) contract awards. Officials reported that, as of September 2011, they were in the process of awarding a contract to develop the system; they estimated it would be operational between September 2012 and January 2013.

Further, SBA regulations require procuring agencies to discuss the requirement's acquisition history, if any, in their 8(a) offer letter and information on any small business contractors which had performed the requirement in the past 2 years.[37] In some cases, however, we found that contracting officers did not include the complete procurement history in their offer letters to SBA even when the requirement had been performed by a prior 8(a) contractor. For one contract we reviewed, the contracting officer had provided no acquisition history in its offer letter to SBA even though he told us that the requirement had previously been performed by the same contractor under another contract awarded by a different agency. He explained that he did not provide the procurement history to SBA because his office had no acquisition history with the requirement. In another example, the contracting officer told SBA there was no acquisition history for the procurement; however, documents in the contract file showed that the agency clearly considered it a follow-on requirement. The contracting officer could not recall why no acquisition history was included in the SBA offer letter, but noted that the scope of work had significantly expanded. SBA district officials also told us that they do not always receive complete procurement history information. In some cases, this is because agency contracting officials are unaware of the full procurement history, which can be a result of contracting officer turnover. Without access to a complete and accurate procurement history, SBA district offices will have difficulty enforcing this new regulation.

SBA Cannot Implement New Rules Intended to Strengthen 8(a) Role in Joint Ventures with Current Information

Non-8(a) businesses can create a mentor-protégé joint venture with an 8(a) firm to win 8(a) prime contracts. In 2006, we reported that there was a risk that large businesses could take advantage of the 8(a) status of firms for their own benefit and that SBA may not obtain the information necessary to determine if the partnership is working as intended.[38] SBA officials told us that they had seen cases where the non-8(a) partner in a joint venture was performing the vast majority—80 to 90 percent—of work on a contract. SBA's new rules require that the 8(a) partner in certain kinds of joint ventures perform a specific portion of the work. Application of this new rule depends on whether the joint venture is *populated* (i.e., it is a separate legal entity that has its own employees) or *unpopulated* (i.e., it merely exists through a written agreement and would use the employees of the 8(a) and non-8(a) partners). The new regulation specifies that the 8(a) partner in (1) an unpopulated joint venture or (2) a populated joint venture with one or more administrative personnel, must perform at least 40 percent of the work performed by the joint venture.

The previous regulations simply stated that the 8(a) partner must perform a "significant portion" of the contract.[39] SBA officials believe that this is an improvement because it gives an exact measure of how much work should be done by the 8(a) partner, to better ensure that the firm receives significant benefit from the venture. However, the agency does not have the information necessary to implement this new requirement.

SBA relies on information from 8(a) firms on their joint venture agreements, but SBA officials told us that they do not always get the information they need to determine how the work would be performed. For example, one joint venture mentor-protégé agreement we reviewed—approved by SBA but formed prior to the new rule—stated that the 8(a) firm would have full responsibility in overseeing performance of any contract awarded to the venture. It further stated that the 8(a) partner would perform at least 51 percent of the work for the contract, but did not provide any details on how the work would be divided. Questions were subsequently raised about this joint venture. In 2008, DCAA—at the request of Army officials who had concerns about the amount of work the tribal 8(a) firm in this joint venture would perform—found that there was not enough financial information available to perform an assessment of either the joint venture or tribal 8(a) firm. DCAA noted, however, that the 8(a) firm had only one employee and that a majority of its work had been subcontracted.[40] An SBA official from the district office overseeing the firm said the agency generally receives an annual statement that a firm is complying with joint venture requirements, but does not receive further information on how the work is split between the 8(a) and non-8(a) partner. SBA officials acknowledge having little insight into how joint venture partners share the work, making it difficult to enforce new regulations.[41]

The new rule also requires that, for populated joint ventures, the non-8(a) firm and its affiliates cannot receive subcontracts at any level—first tier or below—under a joint venture 8(a) contract.[42] For example, the new rule would be violated if a joint venture subcontractor further subcontracted work to a firm that was an affiliate of the non-8(a) partner. Thus, enforcing this rule requires knowledge of all subcontractors at all levels, as well as the ability to identify whether any of the subcontractors are affiliated with the non-8(a) partner. Given SBA's limited insight into subcontracting on 8(a) contracts, this new regulation will be hard to enforce. SBA officials state that they do not see information on planned subcontractors, noting that this information may be included in the contract proposal, which they currently do not review. They also acknowledged that a significant amount of research would be required to uncover any relationship between the non-8(a) firm and all levels of its subcontractors and affiliates. According to SBA headquarters officials, district officials could request contract proposals that would include more information on the planned subcontractors. However, SBA officials do not receive information on changes to the planned subcontractors after contract award.

SBA Has Not Addressed Previously Identified Issues

While the new regulations address certain issues pertaining to the primary and secondary lines of business under which 8(a) firms can operate, the rules' impact on tribal firms, given their special advantages in the program, are not clear. Specifically, SBA has not addressed, in regulation or otherwise, issues we raised in our 2006 report regarding (1) the need for SBA to track the various industries under which multiple 8(a) subsidiaries of one tribal organization are generating revenue and (2) SBA's statutory requirement to determine if firms in a tribal organization will obtain a substantial unfair competitive advantage in an industry.

SBA Still Has Not Addressed Need to Track Revenue Generators

In 2006, we reported that SBA was not tracking the business industries in which ANC subsidiaries won 8(a) contracts under secondary NAICS codes. Thus, SBA was not ensuring that a firm's secondary NAICS codes did not, in effect, become the primary business line under which the firm generated the majority of its revenue. Prior to the recent regulatory changes, if an 8(a) firm outgrew its primary NAICS code, it could still operate in the program and be awarded contracts under one or more of its secondary NAICS codes, as long as it qualified as small for these secondary codes.[43] The new regulations now state that, when an 8(a) participant outgrows the size standard for its primary NAICS code, SBA considers that firm to have met its goals in the program, and SBA may graduate the firm prior to the expiration of its program term. Although this change may shorten the length of time that a tribal 8(a) firm is in the program, its impact is not clear because tribal entities can simply create a new subsidiary with a different stated primary industry, and the subsidiary can continue to work in any industry under secondary NAICS codes.[44] Conversely, non-tribal 8(a) firms can only own one 8(a) firm in a lifetime.

A second regulatory change allows 8(a) participants to change their primary NAICS code if they can show that they have been performing work in a different industry.[45] Previously, the primary NAICS code identified at the time of application was in effect through the firm's tenure in the 8(a) program. For tribal 8(a) firms, this new requirement means that, if they are outgrowing the size standards for their initial primary NAICS code, they can change to a secondary code with larger size standards to stay in the program (as long as it is not the same primary code as a sister subsidiary). However, SBA officials have said that firms will have to show that they are moving into a new industry through a thoughtful process and that outgrowing the size standard cannot be the only reason for changing their industry as this would not be in the spirit of the 8(a) program. At the same time, 8(a) firms are allowed to pursue multiple, diverse lines of business in an unlimited number of secondary NAICS codes. We found that one tribal firm in the 8(a) program had 49 declared NAICS codes, including industrial building construction, investigation services, and religious organizations. Another firm reported 25 different NAICS codes under which it may pursue work, including computer and software stores, advertising agencies, and educational support services.

While the regulatory changes are a step in the right direction in enforcing and enhancing the business development aspects of the program, SBA has not taken steps to address a key finding and recommendation from our 2006 report pertaining to tracking secondary lines of business of 8(a) firms under the same ANC. We reported that SBA was not tracking revenue generated under these firms' secondary lines of business. Thus, SBA was not ensuring that a firm's secondary NAICS codes did not, in effect, become the primary business line by generating the majority of revenue. This situation could allow for a tribal organization to have more than one 8(a) subsidiary perform most of its work under the same primary NAICS code, which SBA regulation does not allow. We recommended that SBA collect data on primary revenue generators for 8(a) ANC firms to ensure that multiple subsidiaries under one parent company were not generating their revenue in the same industry.

SBA systems that track 8(a) participant data do not collect information on the industries in which firms generate their income. In fact, in reviewing annual reports that tribal 8(a) firms had submitted to SBA, we found cases where multiple 8(a) firms under the same tribal entity reported generating most of their revenue in the same industry. For example, SBA records showed that six 8(a) firms under one ANC parent entity generated most of their 2009 revenue in the same lines of business, although each firm has declared a unique primary industry. Table 4 shows the declared primary revenue and actual main revenue generators for 2009 for each subsidiary.

Table 4. Example of the Declared Primary Industries and Actual Revenue Generators of 8(a) Subsidiaries under One ANC Parent Entity

	Declared primary industry	Primary revenue-generating industry, 2009
Subsidiary A	Site preparation contractors	Commercial and institutional building construction
Subsidiary B	Industrial-building construction	Commercial and institutional building construction
Subsidiary C	Facilities support services	Commercial and institutional building Construction
Subsidiary D	Highway, street, and bridge construction	Commercial and institutional building construction
Subsidiary E	Engineering services	Facilities support services
Subsidiary F	Commercial and institutional building construction	Facilities support services

Source: GAO analysis of SBA files.

SBA Has Not Articulated a Process for Addressing the Statutory Requirement to Determine Unfair Competitive Advantage

SBA has not addressed another recommendation we made in 2006 as to how it will comply with an existing law requiring the Administrator to determine whether and when one or more ANC firms are obtaining, or are likely to obtain, a substantial unfair competitive advantage in an industry. "Substantial unfair competitive advantage" is not clearly defined in statute or regulation.[46] We found that the SBA Administrator has never made this determination, nor is there a process in place to do so. Making such a determination would result in all the subsidiaries under a tribal entity being considered affiliated and thus no longer considered independent for size purposes. A finding of affiliation with the parent organization or a sister 8(a) firm could result in a tribal 8(a) firm exceeding small business size standards and not being eligible for 8(a) contracts.

In our current review, we found a few cases where the SBA district office had made such an affiliation determination between tribal 8(a) firms and related non-8(a) firms. In one case, SBA's Alaska district office found affiliation between a tribal 8(a) firm and its part-owner, a business that had previously graduated from the 8(a) program. In another complex situation, a tribal 8(a) firm was 40 percent owned by a large business that was also a subcontractor to one of the 8(a) firm's sister subsidiaries. SBA eventually determined that there was affiliation between the large business and the sister subsidiary, resulting in the two firms' revenues being considered together for the sister firm's size standard determination. As a result, SBA rejected a contract offer for the sister subsidiary where the large business would be a subcontractor, because the firm could not meet the size standards when its revenues were jointly considered with those of the large business. Figure 6 illustrates the relationships between the parent entity, the 8(a) firm and its sister subsidiary, and the large business.

Because SBA has not taken steps to more rigorously determine how to ascertain substantial unfair competitive advantage, there is a risk that tribal 8(a) firms are being considered independent for size determinations when they should be considered affiliated. SBA officials told us that they are in the early stages of drafting a policy that will outline the process for making determinations of unfair competitive advantage.

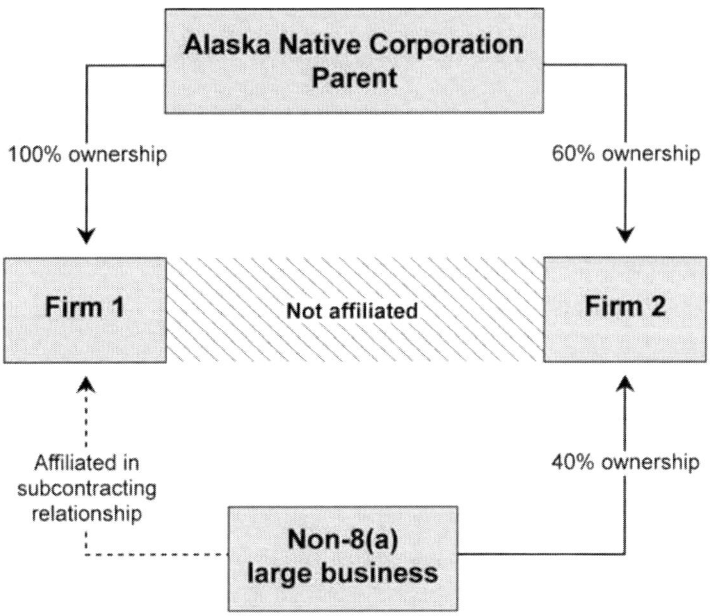

Source: GAO analysis of SBA documentation.

Figure 6. Example of Relationship between Large Business and Tribal 8(a) Firm That Were Found Affiliated.

SBA Has Not Considered Whether Tribal 8(a) Firms' Large Business-Like Practices Are Consistent with the Business Development Purpose of the 8(a) Program

In 2006, SBA officials told us that the charter of ANCs under ANCSA—economic development for Alaska natives from a community standpoint— can be in conflict with the business development intent of the 8(a) program. We pointed out ways that ANCs use the 8(a) program differently than individually owned 8(a) businesses do. Congress has stated that the 8(a) program purpose is exclusively for business development purposes to help small businesses owned and controlled by the socially and economically disadvantaged to compete on an equal basis in the mainstream of the American economy. SBA, in changing its rules to disallow the award of follow-on contracts to tribal 8(a) sister subsidiaries, stated that it expects that two or more firms under the same tribal organization are to operate and grow independently, in line with the business development purposes of the 8(a) program. However, we found other practices, not addressed under the regulations, that highlight the particular nature of tribal 8(a) firms' interconnectedness. These practices result in some firms essentially operating like large businesses and not developing as independent 8(a) firms. For example, the tribal firms often have common management and subcontract with each other or otherwise draw resources from one another or from the parent corporation. Access to these additional resources can help promote their significant business growth over a short period of time, sometimes resulting in firms leaving the 8(a) program early after outgrowing their size standards. By not participating in the transition phase of the program, these firms are missing out on some of the business development aspects of the program, such as competing for non-8(a) contracts to demonstrate their progress in developing into viable businesses that are not solely reliant on the 8(a) program.

SBA headquarters officials recognize that tribal 8(a) firms have some advantages over other 8(a) firms because of the resources they can draw from their parent organization and sister firms. But SBA has not determined whether these other practices we identified are congruent with the business development purpose of the 8(a) program. SBA officials look at individual firms during annual reviews, but do not consider the consequences of their interconnectedness with sister subsidiaries and the parent company in the areas discussed below.

Common Management of Sister Subsidiaries

One way firms under tribal organizations are generally interconnected is through common management. Common management was evident in many of the tribal 8(a) firms' applications we reviewed. For example, the manager of one 8(a) firm also served as Chief Executive Officer to three sister subsidiaries under the same parent, including a sister subsidiary that provides administrative support services to the "family of companies."[47] This practice of common management is a key factor in tribal 8(a) firms' ability to show potential for success in the 8(a) program. SBA requires applicants to show potential for success by having at least 2 years of experience in their primary industry or by showing that their managers have technical and management experience in that industry, among other things. Of the 62 tribal 8(a) firms we reviewed, 44 entered the 8(a) program with less than 2 years of experience in their primary industry. Most of the firms demonstrated potential for success by showing corporate managers' significant experience in the stated primary industry through work with a sister subsidiary. For example, in considering an applicant that was applying to the 8(a) program just 6 months after it was organized, SBA pointed to the extensive managerial and technical experience of the firm's president, including his previous position as vice president to a sister subsidiary. Further, the interconnectivity of some tribal 8(a) firms is also evident where the same board members oversee multiple firms under their parent entity. For example, we found that a member of the board of directors had served on the board of three different 8(a) subsidiaries, while also serving as a member of the board of directors for the parent entity.

Using Sister Subsidiaries for Subcontracting and Past Performance

Another way tribal 8(a) firms become interconnected is through subcontracts with their own sister subsidiaries. During negotiations with the Army for an 8(a) contract, one tribal firm noted its ability to quickly subcontract with its sister firms as a benefit. We found that some tribal firms demonstrated their potential for success when they did not have 2 years in business, using these subcontracts as a record of successful performance in their primary industry. Of the 44 firms we reviewed that entered the program with less than 2 years of experience in their industry, we identified 20 that had obtained some initial experience through subcontracts with a sister subsidiary. For example, we reviewed seven firms owned by one Indian tribe, and five of those seven firms used subcontracts from sister firms to demonstrate their ability to successfully perform work in their primary industry.

As another example of firms' interconnectedness, we found that tribal 8(a) firms can leverage subcontracts from sister subsidiaries to generate required percentages of non-8(a) revenue as the firm progresses in the 8(a) program. During the last 5 years in the program, known as the transition period, firms are required to obtain a certain percentage of non-8(a) revenue to demonstrate their progress in developing a viable business that is not solely reliant on the 8(a) program. In one example, a firm did not meet its non-8(a) revenue requirements in its seventh year in the program. Consequently, the SBA district office placed the firm under remedial action, wherein it was ineligible to receive sole-source 8(a) contracts. However, SBA reinstated the firm after a sister subsidiary awarded it a $20 million subcontract that boosted its non-8(a) revenue to the required annual level. The firm then regained its eligibility to receive sole-source 8(a) contracts.

Tribal 8(a) firms may also cite the past performance of sister firms to demonstrate their own capability to perform under an 8(a) contract. In our review of contract files, we found a number of examples where firms pointed to the past performance of sister subsidiaries in their proposals to demonstrate their capability. One firm, in its business plan presented to SBA, pointed out that leveraging the past performance of a sister company was extremely important as a basis for demonstrating capability to perform. The firm noted that during its first 2 months of operation, it was often asked to provide past performance documentation and that "this is a requirement that is obviously difficult to meet given that we are a brand new company that has only been just recently certified and approved to begin accepting contracts." Another firm pointed out that it had an advantage over competitors because of the history of successful contract performance by sister subsidiaries.

Capitalizing on Corporate Resources and "Brand" to Promote Business

Some tribal 8(a) firms promote the fact that they are part of a larger corporate brand and can access resources from their parent organization and sister firms. Even though tribal 8(a) firms must be "small" under the SBA size standard for their primary industry, their ability to leverage these additional resources can vastly increase the breadth and depth of their capabilities. As the following examples show, the firms can operate, in effect, more like large businesses.

- One ANC 8(a) firm reported to SBA that it is without "geographical limitations as the ANC presence has been established in 49 states.

[The firm] will continue to work with its existing customer base as well as network with agencies familiar with the ANC name."

- One ANC firm reported the intention to transfer staff and management from other subsidiaries as workloads dictate, "with reach back capabilities to access 6,700 employees nationwide and the means of accessing many in-house subject matter experts when necessary." In another contract, the same firm advertised to a procuring agency that its resources included over 7,000 employees at over 90 locations in 31 states to support construction projects. For a different ANC 8(a) firm, procuring agency officials noted that the firm had 4,000 employees it could draw from to perform the contract.
- One firm owned by an Indian tribe, in describing its prior experience, advertised in its proposal to the Army the overall success of firms under the parent entity in providing services to the federal government and managing contract employees. The firm also stated in the proposal that its performance on the contract would be at the same high level as its successful sister firm that had graduated from the 8(a) program, as the firms share the same senior management.
- One ANC has a marketing and proposal services center that is dedicated to supporting all of its subsidiaries in developing cost and technical proposals for government contracts. This ANC also designated an employee to act as the sole point of contact to the SBA for all correspondence and filings for seven of its 8(a) subsidiaries.
- An ANC firm stated in its business plan that a benefit of its organizational structure is the ability to operate as a small company while having access to corporate backing "that typically only a large, seasoned company can provide." Another firm—in its capabilities briefing to a procuring agency—advertised that while the firm is an 8(a) small business, it operates within a resource environment of a large business.
- In its business plan to SBA, an ANC 8(a) firm listed some large businesses as primary competitors in its market, including Lockheed Martin, Northrop Grumman, CACI and General Dynamics.

Tribal 8(a) Firms Can Quickly Outgrow the 8(a) Program

Access to these additional resources, plus the special advantages afforded tribal 8(a) firms, can help promote their significant business growth in the 8(a) program over a short period of time. For example, one tribal 8(a) firm reported average revenues of $31,000 from landscaping contracts when entering the program in 2009. Subsequently, the firm received a $500 million contract for construction. In 2011, the firm reported sales of $21.3 million, an increase of 764 percent from the previous year. In another example, a firm had one employee when it applied to the 8(a) program, but had grown to 124 employees by its first annual review by SBA.

Many tribal 8(a) firms have left the program prior to completing the full 9 year term. Table 5 shows that of the 165 tribal 8(a) firms that have left the program, 70 left prior to completing the full 9 year term. Furthermore, more ANC firms withdrew or graduated from the program early than completed the 9 year term.

For some tribal 8(a) firms, their rapid growth prevents them from reaching the transition phase of the 8(a) program because they have outgrown the small business size standards. The small business regulation states that to ensure participants do not develop an unreasonable reliance on 8(a) awards and to ease their transition into the competitive marketplace after graduating from the 8(a) program, participants must make maximum efforts to obtain business outside the 8(a) program. As a result of withdrawing from the program early, these firms never have to compete for contract awards and thus do not experience some of the intended business development aspects of the 8(a) program. For example:

- In its review of an ANC firm's third year in the 8(a) program, SBA found that the firm had average annual revenue of $78.4 million, which exceeded its small business size standards. Furthermore, SBA pointed out that the firm likely would not meet its targets for non-8(a) revenue once it reached the transition phase and recommended early graduation from the program as a result of these factors. During the firm's time in the program, 99 percent of its revenue came from 8(a) contracts.
- SBA stated in its analysis of another ANC firm's 8(a) application that rapid growth could be a weakness, as subsidiaries under the firm's parent entity tended to grow too large to continue in the 8(a) program after just 4 to 5 years. This firm had reported $318 million in revenue from 8(a) contracts in its third year in the program, and SBA recommended that the firm be graduated early from the program as it was no longer a small business. However, the firm remained in the program for one more year.

Table 5. Summary of Tribal 8(a) Firms That Have Left the Program

	ANC	Indian tribe	NHO	Total
Firms completing full 9 years of program	60	22	3	**85**
Firms that withdrew or graduated early	64	6	0	**70**
Firms that were terminated[a]	5	5	0	**10**
Total firms	**129**	**33**	**3**	**165**

Source: GAO analysis of SBA data.

[a] SBA may terminate a firm's participation in the 8(a) program for a number of reasons, including submitting false information in its 8(a) application and failing to maintain eligibility for program participation.

- In another example, an ANC firm voluntarily withdrew from the 8(a) program after almost 4 years. In commenting to SBA about its experience, the firm suggested that SBA should increase size standards for industries because of the size of large government contracts that tribal firms win.

For tribal 8(a) firms that do continue to the transition phase, some have difficulty meeting non-8(a) revenue requirements because they were awarded large 8(a) sole-source contracts in their early years in the program. In one example, a tribal firm reported to SBA that large 8(a) sole-source contracts were taking up a lot of its existing labor pool, not allowing it to seek non-8(a) contract opportunities. Another firm did not meet its non-8(a) revenue requirements in the transition years, and SBA district officials eventually recommended that this firm voluntarily withdraw as officials believed the firm had not complied with the spirit of the 8(a) program. When a firm does not meet its non-8(a) revenue requirements, it is generally prohibited from receiving further sole-source contracts. However, we found that in 2009, SBA accepted an offer from the Army for a $45 million sole-source award on behalf of a firm that had not met its non-8(a) revenue requirements. SBA district officials thought they may have accepted the offer on behalf of the firm because of severe financial hardship, but they could not locate the file to determine the exact reason.

CONCLUSIONS

It has been more than 20 years since Congress began granting tribal firms special advantages under the 8(a) program. The steady growth in government obligations to these firms, largely through sole-source contracts, draws attention to policies that are designed to promote small businesses and the need to spend taxpayer dollars wisely. SBA has taken some steps, based on our earlier recommendations, to clarify program rules, including the need for monitoring the limitations on subcontracting. However, contracting officers generally are not performing the monitoring—often because of confusion about how to go about doing so and a lack of clarity in existing regulations, particularly with respect to indefinite quantity contracts. Not monitoring the limitations on subcontracting can pose a major risk that an improper amount of work is being done by large business subcontractors under large-dollar value, sole-source contracts to tribal 8(a) firms.

Tribal firms, because of their special advantages in the 8(a) program, can operate under more complex contracts and business relationships than typical 8(a) firms, making oversight difficult. SBA's recent revisions to the 8(a) regulations are intended to address several issues we had raised in the past regarding improved oversight of ANC 8(a) contracting that also apply to all tribal 8(a) firms. However, SBA does not have a way to track the information it needs and lacks clear procedures to deter certain prohibitions addressed in the regulations—for example, sister subsidiaries winning follow-on sole-source contracts and joint-venture partners unduly benefiting from their 8(a) partners' contracts by performing most of the work or improperly subcontracting to an affiliate. The new 8(a) tracking database, which is in the initial stages of development, could, if structured to capture key information, better position SBA to implement these new regulations and to address issues we identified, such as tracking revenues from tribal 8(a) firms' primary and secondary industries. Further, when agencies do not provide the full acquisition history in offer letters, SBA may not have the necessary information to enforce the new regulations. Finally, while SBA officials recently told us they are in the early stages of drafting a policy that will outline a process for determining unfair competitive advantage, SBA still has not addressed in its regulations the process for implementing the statutory requirement to determine whether substantial unfair competitive advantage exists for one or more tribal 8(a) firms.

Finally, some tribal 8(a) firms effectively operate as large firms in a small business program. The practices we have identified, such as capitalizing on corporate resources to promote business and using sister subsidiaries for subcontracting and past performance, are currently allowed, even under SBA's revised regulations. However, it is within SBA's purview as the agency statutorily authorized for the 8(a) program to determine if these practices are congruent with the purpose of the 8(a) program— which is to develop sustainable, small, disadvantaged businesses in the U.S. economy.

RECOMMENDATIONS FOR EXECUTIVE ACTION

To improve oversight of the limitations on subcontracting clause and to clarify who has responsibility for monitoring compliance with the clause, we recommend the Administrator of the Office of Federal Procurement Policy, in consultation with the Administrator of SBA, take the following two actions:

1. Provide specific guidance (including data collection options) to agency officials, including to contracting officers, about how to monitor the extent of subcontracting under 8(a) contracts, including for orders under indefinite quantity contracts.
2. Take actions to amend the FAR to (1) direct contracting officers at agencies that have been delegated responsibility for ensuring compliance with the limitations on subcontracting clause to document in the contract file the steps they have taken to ensure compliance and (2) clarify the percentage of work required by an 8(a) participant under indefinite quantity contracts.

To improve oversight of tribal firms' participation in the 8(a) program, we recommend that the Administrator of SBA take the following five actions:

1. As the new 8(a) tracking database is being developed, take steps to ensure that it has the capability to
   - provide visibility to district offices into all tribal 8(a) firms' activity by tribal entity to ensure compliance with new prohibition to award sole-source 8(a) follow-on contracts to sister subsidiaries;
   - track revenue from tribal 8(a) firms' primary and secondary industry codes to ensure that subsidiaries under the same parent

company are not generating the majority of their revenue from the same primary industry; and

- track information on 8(a) contracts and task or delivery orders, including orders awarded under basic ordering agreements, to help ensure that district officials have information necessary to enforce the 8(a) program regulations.

2. In light of the new prohibition on awarding 8(a) sole-source follow-on contracts to sister subsidiaries, reinforce to procuring agencies the requirement to provide the full acquisition history of the procurement in the offer letter, when available, and direct district office business development specialists to focus on this issue when they review offer letters for tribal 8(a) firms.
3. Establish procedures to enforce new joint venture rules, including how SBA district officials will ascertain that the 8(a) partner performs the required percentage of the joint venture's work and, for populated joint ventures, that the non-8(a) partner and its affiliates do not receive subcontracts under the 8(a) contract.
4. Examine relationships between subsidiaries under tribal entities to determine whether practices such as subcontracting to a sister subsidiary or using the past performance of a sister subsidiary to show capability to perform on an 8(a) contract are in line with the business development purposes of the 8(a) program and should be allowed under program rules. If SBA determines that these practices are not in line with the 8(a) program purposes—and to the extent that Congress has not authorized a practice in law—SBA should address them in its regulations.
5. Establish and communicate to Congress the time frame for developing and implementing SBA's new, planned policy regarding determination of substantial unfair competitive advantage in an industry, and when the policy will be incorporated into the regulations.

AGENCY COMMENTS AND OUR EVALUATION

We provided a draft of this report to SBA; OFPP; the departments of Agriculture, Defense, Energy, Health and Human Services, Homeland Security, Justice, Labor, and State; and the Social Security Administration. We received written comments from SBA. SBA did not address our recommendations. OFPP provided comments on our recommendations via email. The Social Security Administration provided technical comments, which we incorporated as appropriate. The other agencies responded with no comment.

In written comments, SBA provided background information pertaining to the history of Indian tribes' and ANCs' special preferences and their purpose in the 8(a) program. We believe this information is adequately reflected in our report. Although the SBA did not specifically comment on our recommendations, it stated that it will work with us to further strengthen its administration of the 8(a) program. SBA also stated that it will make changes as necessary to continue its efforts to eliminate waste, fraud, and abuse and to ensure that the 8(a) program is operating according to its statutory intent, but did not specify what these actions would entail. In addition, SBA stated that it is fully committed to implementing all of the provisions of its March 2011 regulations, but did not specifically address the issues we raised that may impede such implementation or our related recommendations.

SBA also acknowledged the challenges in administering the 8(a) program with respect to tribal entities because the purpose of including tribally owned entities in the 8(a) program can be contradictory to the program's business development purpose. We recognize in the report that 8(a) businesses owned by tribal entities have special preferences in the program. However, we also note that these entity-owned businesses are subject to the business development purpose of the 8(a) program. This requirement led to our recommendations that SBA determine whether certain practices we found that are currently allowed under the 8(a) regulations—such as firms subcontracting to a sister subsidiary—are consistent with the business development purpose of the 8(a) program.

SBA also commented that its foremost concern with our report was our use of a nonprobability sample, with the suggestion that this sampling technique can be biased based on the judgment of the sampler and that we used this technique to generalize results for tribal 8(a) firms. We strongly disagree. Our use of a nonprobability sample was a sound methodological approach to address our reporting objectives. Nonprobability samples are appropriate to provide illustrative examples or to provide information on a specific group within a population. We used this sampling technique to balance a sample that was large enough to provide a sufficiently comprehensive understanding of the issues with one that was small enough to study within our time and resource constraints. Further, we took a number of steps to ensure the factual accuracy of our findings, including traveling to locations where contract files were located so that we had access to the complete available records and the ability to ask follow-up questions as appropriate to ensure that we did not misinterpret or misrepresent any information in the files. Appendix I of the report sets forth the many steps we took to ensure that our contract file and tribal 8(a) file samples were selected in a non-biased, transparent, and objective manner. In accordance with generally accepted government auditing standards, we appropriately state the results of our work in the report, including the clear statement that our results are not generalizable to the population of tribal 8(a) firms. We did not attempt to generalize our results because that approach was not necessary to meet our objectives.

In an email response, OFPP generally agreed with our recommendations and with our conclusion that steps need to be taken to provide clarity to the acquisition community regarding limitations on subcontracting. OFPP also noted that steps need to be taken to strengthen the application of these requirements to all small business set-aside programs in FAR Part 19. Regarding our recommendation that OFPP provide guidance on how to monitor the extent of subcontracting, OFPP noted that agency officials other than contracting officers—such as agency offices that perform acquisition management reviews and SBA officials—would also be interested parties. We agreed and modified our recommendation to include "agency officials" and not only contracting officers. OFPP stated that it intends to work with the FAR Council and the Chief Acquisition Officers Council to review the roles of various agency officials and evaluate strategies for monitoring and receiving data about the percentage of work performed by a small business prime contractor. It also stated that, with respect to data collection, it anticipates seeking input from the public on strategies to receive and monitor data regarding the percentage of work performed by small business prime contractors. OFPP added that, in taking this action, it intends to minimize the burden on both small businesses and agencies.

OFPP also commented on our recommendation that it take actions to amend the FAR to direct contracting officers to document steps taken to ensure compliance with the limits on subcontracting and to address monitoring requirements for indefinite quantity contracts. OFPP stated that it intends to ask that the FAR Council open a case so that appropriate regulatory refinements may be made to support improvements in the implementation of the limitation on subcontracting. OFPP stated that this action will include reviewing existing clauses that implement the limitation, considering alternatives for collecting information, and documenting steps taken. OFPP also plans to obtain comments from the public, including small businesses, as it develops amendments and evaluates alternatives that can accomplish goals in the least burdensome manner for industry and agencies. Consistent with our recommendation, OFPP plans to clarify in the FAR the percentage of work required by an 8(a) participant under an indefinite quantity contract, but OFPP asked that the recommendation be amended to allow the FAR Council and SBA to work together to determine the best way to clarify this point. We agreed that this would be appropriate and modified the recommendation to reflect this approach.

John P. Hutton
Director
Acquisition and Sourcing Management

APPENDIX I: SCOPE AND METHODOLOGY

The objectives of this review were to (1) identify trends in government 8(a) contracting with firms owned by Alaska Native Corporations (ANC), Native Hawaiian Organizations (NHO), and Indian tribes; (2) determine the reasons federal agencies awarded sole-source contracts to tribal 8(a) firms and the methods used to make price determinations; (3) assess the procuring agencies' oversight of tribal 8(a) contracts for compliance with subcontracting requirements; and (4) examine the Small Business Administration's (SBA) new 8(a) regulation, effective March 14, 2011, to determine how the changes could affect oversight of tribal firms and the extent to which previously identified problems are addressed. In this report, "tribal entities" refers to ANCs, NHOs, and Indian tribes. We use the term "tribal 8(a) firm" to refer to a firm that is majority-owned by an ANC, NHO, or Indian tribe. During the course of our work, we also discussed with procuring agency officials the potential impact of the recent Federal Acquisition Regulation (FAR) requirement for written justifications for sole-source 8(a) awards over $20 million. This requirement was not applicable to the contracts we reviewed. We evaluated the administration of the tribal 8(a) program; the scope of our work did not include an evaluation of the program's merits.

To identify the trends in government tribal 8(a) contracting, we analyzed data from the government's procurement database—the Federal Procurement Data System-Next Generation (FPDS-NG) for fiscal years 2005 through 2010. To assess the reliability of the FPDS-NG we (1) reviewed related documentation, and (2) performed electronic testing on required data fields. We found the FPDS-NG data fields that identify firms owned by ANC, NHO, and Indian tribes to be unreliable because these data were not available during the entire time period. Subsequently, we requested that SBA provide Data Universal Numbering System (DUNS) numbers for 8(a) firms owned by ANC, NHO, and Indian tribes, in addition to mentor-protégé joint ventures that participated in the 8(a) program, for fiscal years 2005 through 2010.[48] We tested the reliability of these DUNS numbers by using them to search for the tribal 8(a) firms and joint ventures in the Central Contractor Registry and SBA's Dynamic Small Business Search database. We used these systems to verify the data SBA had provided, including to identify additional DUNS numbers that were not included among the data SBA had provided. We also requested additional DUNS numbers from SBA on joint ventures with tribal 8(a) firms; however, the information provided was on all joint ventures in the 8(a) program. To select contracts for our sample that were awarded to joint ventures with at least one tribal 8(a) partner, we identified those that had obligations in fiscal year 2009 and then used the Central Contractor Registry to determine whether the joint venture was listed as owned by an ANC, Indian Tribe, or NHO. Once we substituted the compiled final list of DUNS numbers for the tribal 8(a) data fields, we determined that the FPDS-NG was sufficiently reliable to identify trends in tribal 8(a) contracting for fiscal years 2005 through 2010. We adjusted the obligation data for inflation using a gross domestic product price index with a base year of 2010.

To identify the reasons agencies have awarded 8(a) sole-source contracts to firms owned by ANCs, NHOs, and Indian tribes and the methods contracting officials use to determine fair and reasonable price, we selected and reviewed a stratified nonprobability sample of 87 contracts, 7 of which had been competitively awarded. This nonprobability sample was based upon contracts (1) with fiscal year 2009 obligations over the competitive threshold,[49] especially if those obligations exceeded $100 million (fiscal year 2009 data were the most recent at the time) and (2) in locations where multiple tribal 8(a) contracts had been awarded. The majority of the contracts we reviewed (75) were with ANC firms; 10 were with Indian tribes, and 2 were with NHOs. The majority of contracts in our sample (62) were awarded at the Department of Defense (DOD). Our findings from the contract reviews are not generalizable to the population of all tribal 8(a) contracts.

We originally selected 90 contracts for review, 10 of which were coded as competitively awarded. In reviewing the source documentation, we found that two of the contracts had been incorrectly coded: one was not owned by a tribal entity and the other was not awarded through the 8(a) program. We eliminated these contracts from our sample. We also found that obligations under one indefinite quantity contract were listed as two separate contracts in our initial sample; therefore, this was counted as only one contract. Another three contracts had been incorrectly coded in FPDS-NG as competitively awarded or as sole-source. These three contracts remained in our sample.

The specific locations of the contracts in our review were as follows: DOD:

- Air Force Metrology and Calibration, Heath, OH
- National Guard Bureau, Arlington, VA
- Defense Advanced Research Projects Agency, Arlington, VA
- Defense Supply Center, Philadelphia, PA
- Fleet and Industrial Supply Center, Pearl Harbor, HI
- Fort Sam Houston Army Base, TX
- Fort Wainwright Army Base, AK
- Joint Base Elmendorf-Richardson, AK
- Kirtland Air Force Base, NM
- MacDill Air Force Base, FL
- Marine Corps Systems Command, Quantico, VA
- Naval Facilities Engineering Command, Pearl Harbor, HI
- Redstone Arsenal Army Base, AL
- U.S. Army Corp of Engineers locations in Anchorage, AK; Alexandria, VA; Baltimore, MD; Fort Worth, TX; Philadelphia, PA; and Vicksburg, MS
- U.S. Army Research Development and Engineering Command, Natick, MA
- Washington Navy Yard, District of Columbia
- Wright-Patterson Air Force Base, OH

Civilian:

- Department of Agriculture's Forest Service, New Mexico
- Department of Energy's National Nuclear Security Administration-Service Center, New Mexico
- Department of Health and Human Service's Centers for Disease Control and Prevention Atlanta, GA; Centers for Medicare and

Medicaid Services, Baltimore, MD; and Food and Drug Administration, Rockville, MD
- Department of Homeland Security's Bureau of Customs and Border Protection, Federal Emergency Management Agency, and Office of Procurement Operations, Washington, D.C.
- Department of Justice's Drug Enforcement Administration, Washington, D.C., and Federal Bureau of Investigation, Chantilly, VA
- Department of Labor's Office of Procurement Services, Washington, D.C.
- Department of State's Office of Acquisition Management, Arlington, VA
- Social Security Administration's Office of Acquisition and Grants, Baltimore, MD.

For the contracts in our sample, we examined contract file documentation, including acquisition plans, market research reports, and price negotiation memorandums. However, for three of the contracts we reviewed, one each at the Army Corps, Department of Homeland Security, and the State Department, pre-award information was completely missing from the files. For one of these, we were unable to determine whether or not it had been competitively awarded, as coded in FPDS-NG, because of the missing information. We also interviewed contracting officials, small business advocates, and program officials.

To determine the extent to which procuring agencies are overseeing tribal 8(a) contracts for compliance with the 8(a) program's subcontracting requirements, we reviewed and analyzed documentation for the contracts in our review, including acquisition plans, price negotiation memorandums, contractor proposals, and SBA offer and acceptance letters, in addition to any additional information pertaining to subcontractor monitoring. We also interviewed contracting and program officials, as well as agency small business advocates, about the methods they employ to monitor compliance. Additionally, we reviewed agency- specific guidance or operating instructions, various statutory provisions, the Federal Acquisition Regulation, and Title 13 of the Code of Federal Regulations. We also drew from the findings in our 2006 report on 8(a) contracting with ANC firms.[50]

To determine the extent to which SBA's new regulations could affect oversight of tribal firms' participation in the 8(a) program and to which previously identified problems have been addressed, we reviewed SBA documents, such as annual reviews and 8(a) program applications, for selected tribal firms. These firms were strategically chosen based upon their parent entity's (i.e., ANC, NHO, or Indian tribe) representation in our overall contract sample. We selected those firms whose parent entities had higher representation in our sample and those with less representation. Consequently, we examined the files for 49 ANC, 3 NHO, and 10 Indian tribe firms. For the ANC firms, the 49 firms fell under 11 parent entities. The results of our review are not generalizable to the population of tribal 8(a) firms. Moreover, we reviewed SBA regulations, operating procedures and business systems (such as the system used to process 8(a) applications), and interviewed officials at SBA headquarters and the Alaska, Hawaii, Oklahoma, New Mexico, and Washington, D.C., district offices. We also met or spoke with ANC, NHO, and Indian tribe representatives in three "town hall" meetings to explain the scope and methodology for this review. We did not assess the extent to which benefits from tribal 8(a) contracts flow to the parent entity.

We conducted this performance audit from October 2010 to January 2012 in accordance with generally accepted government auditing standards. Those standards require that we plan and perform the audit to obtain sufficient, appropriate evidence to provide a reasonable basis for our findings and conclusions based on our audit objectives. We believe that the evidence obtained provides a reasonable basis for our findings and conclusions based on our audit objectives.

End Notes

[1] The goal of the Act was, in part, to resolve long-standing aboriginal land claims and to foster economic development for Alaska Natives. ANCs are eligible to participate in federal procurement programs, such as the 8(a) program, pursuant to ANCSA. See 43 U.S.C. §§ 1602, 1626(a) and (e).

[2] GAO, *Contract Management: Increased Use of Alaska Native Corporations' Special 8(a) Provisions Calls for Tailored Oversight*, GAO-06-399 (Washington, D.C.: Apr. 27, 2006). For example, legislative language suggests that 8(a) businesses owned by Indian tribes and ANCs were exempt from sole source dollar thresholds because such businesses are located on reservations and account for the major employment of the workforce. ANCs, however, do not have reservations.

[3] 13 C.F.R. § 124.1. (1989) The regulations were revised in 1998 to restate the business development purpose of the program for "small disadvantaged business concerns," which include tribal 8(a) firms.

[4] FAR 6.303-1(b). The written justification must be approved in writing by the appropriate official depending on the dollar value (see FAR 6.304) and made publicly available (see FAR 6.305).

[5] National Defense Authorization Act for Fiscal Year 2010, § 811 (2009).

[6] Our initial sample included 90 contracts; however, we excluded 2 from the sample because they had been incorrectly coded in FPDS-NG as being awarded through the 8(a) program to tribal 8(a) firms. A third contract was excluded because obligations under one indefinite quantity contract had been listed in FPDS-NG as being under two separate contracts.

[7] GAO-06-399.

[8] The NAICS assigns codes to all economic activity within 20 broad sectors, and the codes reflect the industry in which the firm operates, e.g., wireless telecommunication carriers or industrial building construction. SBA has designated a small business size standard for every NAICS code. Applicants to the 8(a) program must qualify as small under their primary NAICS code at the time of application and SBA's certification date. SBA regulation requires that at least 2 years lapse after a tribal firm exits the 8(a) program before another firm owned by the same parent entity can enter the program with the prior firm's primary NAICS code.

[9] FAR 19.804-2.

[10] For agencies where there is no partnership agreement in place, SBA is generally responsible for the contract administration function.

[11] SBA must approve the mentor/protégé agreement before the two businesses submit an offer as a joint venture to receive exclusion from affiliation. 13 C.F.R. §§ 124.513(b)(3) and 124.520(b) and (d)(1)(i).

[12] GAO-06-399.

[13] Interestingly, this trend is the opposite of what we reported in 2010 regarding obligations under all contracts (not just those awarded to 8(a) firms). We found that the majority of noncompetitive obligations from fiscal years 2006 to 2009 occurred in the first quarter of the fiscal year. GAO, *Federal Contracting: Opportunities Exist to Increase Competition and Assess Reasons When Only One Offer is Received*, GAO-10-833 (Washington, D.C.: July 26, 2010).

[14] GAO-06-399.

[15] The federal government has an annual agencywide goal of awarding not less than 23 percent of all prime contract dollars to small businesses. See 15 U.S.C. § 644(g)(1).

[16] SBA may not accept a procurement into the 8(a) program under certain circumstances and if the contract pricing exceeds a fair market price.

[17] We recently reported on opportunities to strengthen acquisition planning. See GAO, *Acquisition Planning: Opportunities to Build Strong Foundations for Better Service Contracts,* GAO-11-672 (Washington, D.C.: Aug. 9, 2011).

[18] The A-76 process is a federal government policy which subjects commercial activities to competition and requires agency officials to identify all activities performed by government personnel as either commercial or inherently governmental. OMB, *Circular A-76 (Revised), Performance of Commercial Activities* 4, (May 29, 2003). The provisions in these appropriations acts allowed DOD to avoid the A-76 process when contracting with tribal 8(a) firms. DOD used the authority in section 8(a) of the Small Business Act to make the sole source awards. See, for example, Consolidated Security, Disaster Assistance, and Continuing Appropriations Act, 2009, Pub. L. No. 110-329 § 8016, 122 Stat. 3623-24 (Sept. 30, 2008).

[19] A BOA is a written instrument of understanding between an agency and contractor that generally contains terms and clauses applying to future orders, a description of supplies and services to be provided, and methods for pricing future orders under the BOA. FAR 16.703(a).

[20] This type of contract provides for an indefinite quantity, within stated limits, of supplies or services during a fixed period. The government places orders for individual requirements. Quantity limits may be stated as number of units or as dollar values.

[21] As examples, 8(a) sole-source awards to tribal 8(a) firms have been protested in *Mission Critical Solutions*, B-401057, May 4, 2009 and *JMX, Inc.*, B-402643, June 25, 2010.

[22] A sister subsidiary is another tribal 8(a) firm that is owned by the same parent entity.

[23] GAO bid protest decisions have established that an agency may consider the experience or past performance of an offeror's parent or affiliated company under certain circumstances, for instance where the proposal demonstrates that the resources of the parent or affiliate will affect contract performance. However, reliance on a third party's experience, even if otherwise permissible, could be precluded from consideration by a solicitation provision.

[24] GAO-10-833. We also recently reported on the program offices' roles in acquisition planning (GAO-11-672).

[25] All of the contracts in our sample were awarded prior to the March 2011 effective date of SBA's new regulations, which now prohibit the award of a follow-on sole source 8(a) contract to an Indian tribe or ANC sister subsidiary under the same tribal entity.

[26] DCAA provides services that can help DOD and other federal agencies by performing audits and providing financial advisory services in connection with the negotiation, administration, and settlement of contracts and subcontracts.

[27] GAO-10-833 and GAO, *Opportunities to Reduce Potential Duplication in Government Programs, Save Tax Dollars, and Enhance Revenue,* GAO-11-318SP (Washington, D.C.: Mar. 1, 2011).

[28] See GAO, *Federal Contracting: OMB's Acquisition Savings Initiative Had Results, but Improvements Needed,* GAO-12-57 (Washington, D.C.: Nov. 15, 2011) for our observations on an OMB initiative to reduce spending under high-risk contracts, including noncompetitive awards and awards receiving only one offer.

[29] 13 C.F.R § 125.6(a)(1); FAR 52.219-14, "Limitations on Subcontracting."

[30] GAO-06-399.

[31] In one contract file we reviewed at the Department of Energy, the contractor's invoices reflected the amount of work that was subcontracted; however, there was no evidence that agency officials were actively monitoring the subcontracting limitations. For an Army contract in our sample, contracting officials told us they started monitoring the amount of work that was subcontracted after their Principal Assistant Responsible for Contracting directed them to do so; until that time, the limitations on subcontracting had not been monitored.

[32] In another report, we recommended that SBA incorporate regular assessments of 8(a) contracting into its surveillance reviews that monitor small business contracting at federal agencies. This would include assessing how agencies administer and oversee 8(a) contracting under the partnership agreements. See GAO, *Small Business Administration: Agency Should Assess Resources Devoted to Contracting and Improve Several Processes in the 8(a) Program,* GAO-09-16, (Washington, D.C.: Nov. 21, 2008).

[33] SBA regulations provide that, through special contract clauses in the 8(a) contract documents or by separate agreement, SBA may delegate to procuring activities responsibility for certain contract administration matters. 13 C.F.R. § 124.512.

[34] SBA regulations require 8(a) firms to certify in their offers that they will meet the applicable percentage of work requirement for each contract when subcontracting. However, for agencies with partnership agreements, monitoring compliance with the limitations on subcontracting clause after contract award is the procuring agency's responsibility. As noted above, for all of the agencies in our review, SBA has delegated responsibility for contract administration to the contracting officers through partnership agreements.

[35] For supply or service contracts, this 50 percent minimum requirement does not apply to work performed under each individual task order, nor does it oblige a contractor to meet the required percentages cumulatively for work performed under all task orders at any given point in time during the contract's life. 13 CFR § 124.510 (c).

[36] NHOs are also subject to the new prohibition; however, it applies only 2 years from the date on which the firms have been admitted to the 8(a) program.

[37] These regulations were in place prior to the revisions in SBA's 2011 final rule and were used to determine if other small businesses would be adversely impacted by accepting the requirement into the 8(a) program. 13 CFR § 124.502(c)(9) and 13 CFR § 124.502(c)(10).

[38] GAO-06-399. In another report, also issued in 2006, we found that SBA had not carried out its responsibilities to monitor an 8(a) joint venture, mentor/protégé partnership that had won a $354 million sole source contract where the protégé firm did not appear to be getting the beneficial experience expected. See GAO, *State Department Contract Awarded for Security Installation at Embassies Awarded to 8(a) Joint Venture*, GAO-07-33R (Washington, D.C.: Nov. 8, 2006).

[39] While the new rule specifies that the 8(a) partner in a populated joint venture with administrative personnel must perform at least 40 percent of the work, the new rule does not address the amount of work the 8(a) partner must perform in a joint venture populated with employees intended to actually perform the contract work. For these joint ventures, the 8(a) participant must demonstrate what it will gain from performance of the contract and how this will assist in its business development. The new rule also states that the 8(a) participant must demonstrate that it controls the joint venture. 13 CFR § 124.513 (d)(1).

[40] SBA records we reviewed showed that the 8(a) firm had grown to almost 100 employees in 2010.

[41] The new SBA rules require the 8(a) participant in a joint venture to annually, and at contract completion, describe how it is meeting or has met the performance of work requirements for 8(a) contracts performed as a joint venture. However, SBA officials did not explain whether or how they will use this reporting requirement to ensure compliance with the new regulations.

[42] The final rule provides an exception to this rule if SBA determines that other potential subcontractors are not available, or the joint venture is populated only with administrative personnel.

[43] A firm outgrows its primary NAICS code when it exceeds the size standard for that NAICS code for three successive program years.

[44] New tribal 8(a) firms cannot operate under the same primary NAICS code as a sister firm that has already been admitted to the program or that graduated within the last 2 years.

[45] This is demonstrated when a majority of a firm's revenues during a 2-year period has evolved from its former primary code to another code in a different industry.

[46] 15 U.S.C. § 636(j)(1)(J)(ii)(II) and 13 C.F.R. § 124.109(c)(2)(iii).

[47] Federal laws provide that a tribal 8(a) firm may own more than one firm eligible for assistance from the 8(a) program if, among other things, the individuals responsible for the management and daily operations of the concern do not manage more than two program participants. We did not assess whether these individuals met the requirements for management and control of the daily operations of the tribal 8(a) firm.

[48] A DUNS number is a 9-digit identification number assigned by Dun & Bradstreet, Inc., to identify unique business entities.

[49] The competitive 8(a) threshold is $6.5 million for manufacturing or $4 million for all other acquisitions.

[50] GAO, *Contract Management: Increased Use of Alaska Native Corporations' Special 8(a) Provisions Calls for Tailored Oversight*, GAO-06-399 (Washington, D.C.: Apr. 27, 2006).

In: Federal Contracting
Editor: Gail Nelson

ISBN: 978-1-53610-367-0

Chapter 2

ALASKA NATIVE CORPORATIONS: OVERSIGHT WEAKNESSES CONTINUE TO LIMIT SBA'S ABILITY TO MONITOR COMPLIANCE WITH 8(A) PROGRAM REQUIREMENTS*

United States Government Accountability Office

WHY GAO DID THIS STUDY

Federal obligations under SBA's 8(a) Business Development Program totaled about $4 billion for 344 ANC- owned firms in 2014. In 2011, SBA updated program regulations to address prior oversight challenges identified by GAO. GAO was asked to follow-up on past reports and examine SBA's current oversight processes. This report discusses, among other things, SBA's ability to (1) enforce regulations prohibiting the award of follow-on, sole-source 8(a) contracts to subsidiaries of the same ANC; (2) limit subsidiaries of the same 8(a) ANC from operating in the same primary line of business, and (3) address challenges, if any, to SBA's oversight of 8(a) ANC-owned firms. To do this work, GAO analyzed fiscal year 2011 through 2014 data from a federal contracting database using separate nongeneralizable samples for each

* This is an edited, reformatted and augmented version of the United States Government Accountability Office publication, GAO-16-113, dated March 2016.

objective, conducted site visits, reviewed 8(a) sole-source contracts, and ANC-owned firm annual updates, and interviewed relevant SBA officials.

What GAO Recommends

GAO recommends that, among other things, SBA asks other federal agencies to specifically identify whether a contract is a follow-on in their letters to SBA; develop plans and timelines for tracking ANC-owned firms' revenues across lines of business; and enable its staff to access and share relevant revenue data. SBA agreed with two recommendations and reported actions taken to implement two others. SBA disagreed with the final two, stating they were unnecessary. Based on a review of actions taken, GAO believes all six recommendations are still warranted.

What GAO Found

GAO has reported in the past that the Small Business Administration's (SBA) ability to enforce regulations prohibiting the award of follow-on, sole-source contracts to 8(a) subsidiary firms of the same Alaska Native Corporation (ANC) relies on contract information from other federal agencies that is sometimes incomplete. SBA's regulations prohibit program participants from receiving an 8(a) sole-source contract that immediately follows another 8(a) contract with the same requirements performed by another participant owned by the same ANC. Other federal agencies offering 8(a) contracts must generally submit offer letters to SBA that include information about a contract's procurement history and name of any prior small business contractors. SBA relies on this information to determine whether a firm is eligible to receive a particular 8(a), follow-on, sole- source contract. However, GAO's analysis of a selection of contracts for this review found that agencies are not required to directly identify whether a sole- source contract is also a follow-on contract in these letters. One SBA office has begun taking action to address this limitation by asking agencies to specifically report whether contracts are follow-on, sole-source awards in offer letters, but the change has not been broadly adopted. SBA would be better positioned to limit the award of follow-on, sole-source contracts by ANC-owned subsidiaries if it requested that other federal agencies specifically state whether contracts are follow-ons in offer letters.

GAO found in past reports and this review and in that SBA's ability to enforce its regulation prohibiting subsidiaries owned by the same ANC from operating in the same primary line of business as reported to SBA is hindered by limited tracking and sharing of information across SBA's 68 district offices. ANC-owned firms must register a primary line of business with SBA, but are allowed to pursue multiple other lines of business. In this review, GAO found 5 of 39 ANCs owned subsidiaries that generated a greater portion of revenues in secondary lines of business than their registered primary line of business. Additionally, those secondary lines of business were the same lines of business as the primary lines for other subsidiaries owned by the same ANC. Such activity could potentially conflict with the regulation's intent. SBA proposed a rule designed to limit and track this activity, but lacks plans and timelines associated with this effort. Regarding limited information-sharing, different district offices service different firms that are subsidiaries of the same ANC. Oversight staff in these offices cannot access or share relevant data from other district offices. Without better data sharing, SBA cannot monitor whether firms owned by the same ANC and serviced by different district offices are complying with program rules.

As GAO reported in the past, SBA's staffing for its data collection and program guidance activities contributed to weak program oversight and monitoring of 8(a) ANC-owned firms. SBA took some recent actions to enhance oversight, such as conducting an accountability review in October 2014 of the Alaska District Office. SBA has established an office to improve compliance with 8(a) rules by verifying self-reported information supplied by firms. However, SBA does not have plans that detail the office's roles and responsibilities for its activities. With the oversight weaknesses GAO identified in this review, SBA has an opportunity to enhance its oversight by finalizing plans for this office.

ABBREVIATIONS

ANC	Alaska Native Corporation
BDMIS	Business Development Management Information System
DPCE	Division of Program Certification and Eligibility
DSBS	Dynamic Small Business Search
FAR	Federal Acquisition Regulation
FPDS-NG	Federal Procurement Database System-Next Generation
GSA	General Services Administration

OIG	Office of Inspector General
NAICS	North American Industry Classification System
SAM	System for Award Management
SAP	Simplified Acquisition Procedures
SBA	Small Business Administration
VERA	Voluntary Early Retirement Authority
VSIP	Voluntary Separation Incentive Payments

***

March 21, 2016

The Honorable Claire McCaskill
Ranking Member
Permanent Subcommittee on Investigations
Committee on Homeland Security and Governmental Affairs
United States Senate

The Honorable Edward J. Markey
United States Senate

The Honorable Peter DeFazio
House of Representatives

The 8(a) Business Development Program (8[a] program), administered by the Small Business Administration (SBA), is one of the federal government's primary vehicles for developing socially and economically disadvantaged small businesses, including those firms owned by Alaska Native Corporations (ANC.)[1] One of the key benefits of the program is the ability of participants to receive federal contract awards set aside solely for 8(a) firms. Government agencies obligated about $17 billion to just under 5,600 firms participating in SBA's 8(a) program in fiscal year 2014.[2] Obligations to ANC-owned firms participating in the 8(a) program represent a sizeable share of total obligations made to all firms participating in the program. For fiscal year 2014, federal obligations under the program totaled about $4 billion for 344 8(a) ANC-owned firms and represented almost a quarter of all 8(a) obligations made that year.

Congress has provided ANC-owned firms participating in the 8(a) program with distinct advantages over most other participating firms, including provisions exempting them from some of SBA's standard 8(a) program eligibility requirements and an authorization to receive sole- source 8(a) contracts for any amount.[3] Generally, for a firm to participate in the 8(a) program, SBA must certify that the firm meets several criteria, including that it is a small business as defined by SBA and is unconditionally owned and controlled by one or more socially and economically disadvantaged individuals. However, program rules allow firms that are majority owned by ANC parent entities to be considered eligible for the 8(a) program as long as they can attest to being a small business individually.[4] Further, ANC-owned firms are also allowed contract flexibilities not afforded to most other 8(a) participants. For example, under the 8(a) program, contracts generally can be awarded to participating small businesses without competition (known as sole-source contracts) when valued below $4 million—including any options—or $6.5 million for manufacturing contracts. There is also typically a limit on the total dollar value of sole-source contracts that 8(a) firms can receive while in the program—$100 million or five times the size standard corresponding to the firm's primary line of business. 8(a) ANC-owned firms are exempt from these limits. Federal procuring departments and agencies are allowed to make sole-source awards of any size to 8(a) ANC-owned firms and these firms may continue to receive awards once the total dollar value threshold that applies to other 8(a) firms of $100 million has been exceeded.

In February 2011, SBA issued new and updated existing regulations that were partly designed to prohibit certain behaviors by firms participating in the 8(a) program.[5] For example, the updated regulations preclude sister firms from receiving (and, therefore, agencies from awarding) follow-on, sole-source contracts—that is, the prohibited practice of awarding subsequent contracts with essentially the same requirements to sister subsidiary firms of the same parent ANC. The changes also included technical changes to existing rules that dictate how the agency monitors the participation of ANC-owned firms in the same lines of business, and provided clarifying language to existing rules related to compensation. In addition, SBA issued a new rule that requires ANC-owned firms to report how the benefits from 8(a) program participation are distributed to Alaska natives or their community.

However, in January 2012, we reported that, even with changes to its regulations, SBA lacked critical data it needed to implement or enforce compliance with some of the new or existing 8(a) program requirements, including prohibitions against awarding follow-on, sole-source contracts to subsidiary 8(a) firms owned by the same ANC, as well as tracking the participation of firms in the same lines of business.[6] In that report, we stated that if SBA did not take steps to strengthen its program controls, ANC 8(a) firms and others could remain in the program in perpetuity— they could shift the management of one subsidiary to another to receive follow-on contracts or circumvent the prohibition against sister subsidiaries operating in the same primary line of business. We recommended, among other things, that SBA

1. enhance its technological capacity by providing visibility to district offices into all tribal 8(a) firms' activity by tribal entity to ensure compliance with the new prohibition on awarding follow-on, sole-source 8(a) contracts to sister subsidiaries;
2. track revenue by ANC-owned firms' industry codes to ensure that subsidiaries participating in the program and under the same parent company are not generating the majority of their revenue from the same primary industry; and
3. reinforce, to procuring agencies, the requirement to provide the full acquisition history of the procurement in the offer letter, when available, and direct district office business development specialists to focus on this issue when reviewing contract offers made to ANC-owned firms.[7]

You asked us to examine SBA's oversight of ANC 8(a) contracts. This report discusses the extent to which: (1) SBA enforces its regulations prohibiting the award of follow-on, sole-source 8(a) contracts to subsidiaries of the same ANC; (2) SBA limits subsidiaries of the same ANC from operating in the same primary line of business; (3) information is known about compensation, revenues, and benefits distribution of ANC-owned firms; and (4) SBA has addressed challenges, if any, to its oversight and monitoring of ANC-owned firms participating in the 8(a) program since 2011.[8] This report exclusively discusses these issues in the context of ANC-owned firms participating in the 8(a) program.

For the analyses performed in all objectives, we reviewed 8(a) program information on ANC firms participating in the program from fiscal year 2011 through fiscal year 2014 to reflect the effective date of regulations included in our scope. To perform our work we used the Federal Procurement Database System–Next Generation (FPDS-NG) to select three sets of cases of ANC-owned firms that met certain criteria specific to our objectives, which we outline in detail below.[9] To assess the reliability of the FPDS-NG data, we interviewed officials who maintain the database, reviewed related documentation, and tested the data for missing or erroneous values. Where possible, we also tested these data against other datasets maintained by SBA and the General Services Administration (GSA).[10] During the course of our review, we identified a few data limitations with FPDS-NG, such as misclassified 8(a) firms and incorrect obligations. To mitigate these limitations, we interviewed knowledgeable individuals about the contracts in question and corrected errors we identified. We found the data to be sufficiently reliable for the purpose of selecting cases for review (see appendix I for additional details on the data's reliability). As described in the following sections, we selected a subset of cases for each objective that met certain criteria for follow-up review and illustrative examples, and therefore our findings are not generalizable to the entire population of ANCs participating in the 8(a) program.

To identify the extent to which SBA enforces its regulations prohibiting the award of follow-on, sole-source 8(a) contracts to subsidiaries of the same ANC, we assessed the agency's policies and procedures related to these processes, and interviewed cognizant staff. We analyzed FPDS-NG to identify 8(a) sole-source contracts that were awarded during the fiscal year period 2011 through 2014. Because there is no federal database that specifically identifies follow-on, sole-source contracts, we looked for certain contract characteristics in FPDS-NG that were an indication of a potential follow-on to a sister-subsidiary. We identified contracts that had the following characteristics: (1) ANC-owned firms that shared the same parent ANC, location, and work performed by firms and sister subsidiaries; and (2) contracts with sequential award dates. On the basis of this analysis, we identified 155 contracts overall—about 4 percent of all contracts awarded to ANC-owned 8(a) firms from fiscal year 2011 through 2014—that could have been potential follow-on, sole-source contracts according to our FPDS-NG data. We randomly selected 53 of these contracts for further review. The 53 contracts represented two groups: 23 small-value contracts (those contracts valued at $150,000 or less), and 30 large-value contracts (those contracts valued at more than $150,000). Because, generally, agencies are not required to provide offer letters to SBA prior to the award of contracts that are $150,000 or less, our analysis ultimately focused on the 30 large-value contracts.[11] For these 30 large-value contracts, we reviewed documents such as offer letters and the actual contracts. Our review did not identify any contracts that were also follow-on, sole-source contracts. Table 1 outlines our selection of the sole-source contracts awarded from fiscal year 2011 through 2014

Table 1. Summary of Selected Sole-Source Contracts, 2011–2014

Contract Type	Contract Characteristics
30 large value contracts[a]	Contracts valued at more than $150,000. Files must contain documents such as offer letters and awarded contracts.
23 small value contracts	Contracts valued at $150,000 or less Prior notification to SBA not required.[b]

Source: GAO analysis | GAO-16-113

Note: The random selection was taken from 155 contracts initially identified as potential follow-on, sole-source contracts based on selected variables.

[a] This report's final analysis focused on these large-value contracts.

[b] For this reason, these 23 contracts were excluded from our analysis.

Because of the imprecision in using these variables to identify the population of follow-on, sole-source contracts—that is, we cannot be fully assured that we have identified all possible cases—the results of our analysis are not generalizable to the larger population of contracts we identified. Further, it was not possible to determine from FPDS-NG data alone whether the other remaining 102 contracts that we initially identified in FPDS-NG as potential follow-on, sole-source contracts were actually follow-on, sole-source contracts. Such a determination can only be made by a detailed review of each of the cases.[12]

To evaluate the extent to which SBA limits 8(a) subsidiaries of the same ANC from operating in the same primary line of business—that is, operating businesses primarily within the same North American Industry Classification System (NAICS) code—we reviewed SBA policies, guidance, and procedures in place at the time of our audit.[13] We also analyzed subsidiary data from three systems: FPDS-NG, the System for Award Management (SAM), and SBA's Dynamic Small Business Search (DSBS).[14] Using these systems, we selected a non-generalizable selection of 39 unique parent ANCs that each owned multiple subsidiaries that participated in the 8(a) program and generated at least $1 in 8(a) contract obligations from fiscal year 2011 through 2014.[15] We reviewed detailed information on these 39 ANCs. To verify the accuracy of data taken from these systems, we interviewed 6 ANC parent companies about the accuracy of data elements relevant to our findings, including NAICS codes, 8(a) program entrance and exit dates, obligations and revenue amounts. Additionally, because there were a number of new initiatives that SBA introduced related to this objective, we used our past guidance to assess whether the plans that SBA had in place articulated a results orientation, used intermediate steps to indicate progress made toward achieving its goals, and addressed identified mission critical goals.[16] Our findings under this objective are not generalizable to the entire population of ANC-owned firms participating in the 8(a) program.

To determine the extent to which information is known regarding compensation, revenue, and benefit distribution of 8(a) ANC-owned firms, we randomly selected 30 firms that FPDS-NG identified as ANC-owned subsidiary firms active in the 8(a) program from fiscal year 2011 through 2014.[17] We excluded four firms from our analysis because our review revealed that they were other than ANC-owned firms.[18] We reviewed files (including applications and annual updates) for the 26 selected ANC- owned firms. Much of the data that we reviewed for this section were self- reported by ANC subsidiaries. We interviewed district office officials to discuss preliminary results from our file review and reviewed related documentation. Additionally, we spoke with officials from three associations about their knowledge of compensation paid by ANC-owned 8(a) firms. These groups represent the interests of the chief executive officers from the 12 Native Regional Corporations; that address issues related to Native federal contracting; and another group that represents the interests of indigenous people, generally. We also present information collected on subsidiary firm ownership in appendix II. Our description of firms under this objective is not generalizable to the entire population of ANC-owned firms participating in the 8(a) program.

To assess the extent to which SBA has addressed challenges, if any, to its oversight and monitoring of ANC-owned firms participating in the 8(a) program since 2011, we reviewed SBA's implementation of program mechanisms designed to ensure the compliance of regulations related to our scope of work. We reviewed relevant SBA controls, policies, procedures, and guidance, and assessed the extent to which these mechanisms effectively aligned with federal standards for internal controls.[19] We also interviewed key SBA officials and staff located at headquarters and at 4 of the 68 SBA district offices including Anchorage, Alaska; Richmond, Virginia; Washington, D.C.; and San Francisco, California, regarding SBA's implementation of management controls relevant to the scope of our review. These offices were selected because of the role they play in the 8(a) program (such as the San Francisco office's role in certifying the initial applications for ANC-owned firms seeking to enter the program) or for the number of ANC 8(a) firms that they service. For example, we selected a district office that served a large number of ANC-owned firms (the Alaska District Office) and ones that served a smaller number of firms (e.g. Washington, D.C., and Richmond, Virginia district offices) to compare their practices. We conducted site visits to both the

Anchorage, Alaska, and Washington, D.C., district offices. During these site visits, we interviewed staff and conducted file reviews of selected ANC subsidiaries serviced by those district offices. As a part of our site visit to SBA's district office in Anchorage, Alaska, we collected data related to SBA's human capital planning for that office. Our approach to this specific part of the engagement included reviewing documents and interviewing cognizant officials with expertise in workforce planning methods. During these interviews, we discussed workforce plans, historical and current staffing numbers, and related challenges. Specifically, we asked about the skills and competencies needed to achieve program results, discussed the agency's strategies to address staffing gaps, and building necessary capacity. Additionally, we reviewed our own past work on human capital issues for guidance.[20] To inform other aspects of this objective, we also attended an SBA tribal consultation in Anchorage, Alaska, to obtain the overall perspectives of ANCs and their subsidiary firms on the 2011 regulatory changes to the program. The findings from these site visits and interviews are not generalizable to the other SBA district offices. Additional details on our scope and methodology for each objective can be found in appendix I.

We conducted this performance audit from May 2014 to March 2016 in accordance with generally accepted government auditing standards. Those standards require that we plan and perform the audit to obtain sufficient, appropriate evidence to provide a reasonable basis for our findings and conclusions based on our audit objectives. We believe that the evidence obtained provides a reasonable basis for our findings and conclusions based on our audit objectives.

BACKGROUND

8(a) Business Development Program

The 8(a) program was designed to assist small, disadvantaged businesses in competing in the American economy through business development. Over the course of the program, qualified small, disadvantaged businesses can receive business development support from SBA, such as mentoring, procurement assistance, business counseling, training, financial assistance, surety bonding, and other management and technical assistance. However, one of the key areas of support is eligibility for set-aside competitive and sole-source federal contracts for 8(a) businesses, which can be an important factor in the financial development for ANC-owned firms.[21]

Organizational Structure

Generally, ANCs as organizations can be either for-profit or not-for-profit and can own a family of for-profit subsidiary firms, including but not limited to, wholly-owned holding companies that often provide administrative support to smaller sister subsidiaries.[22] Additionally, ANCs can wholly or partially own, with at least a majority share, the subsidiary firms that participate in the 8(a) program, as illustrated in Figure 1. But one condition for participation in the 8(a) program is that subsidiary firms are for-profit. Appendix II contains additional descriptive information about ownership for the firms we selected for our review.

According to program rules, once a firm has been certified to participate in the 8(a) program, any changes in ownership should be reported to the local SBA district office.[23] When a change in ownership is reported, SBA's certification and program eligibility office in San Francisco reevaluates that firm's eligibility. SBA relies on the firm to provide updates on changes in ownership.

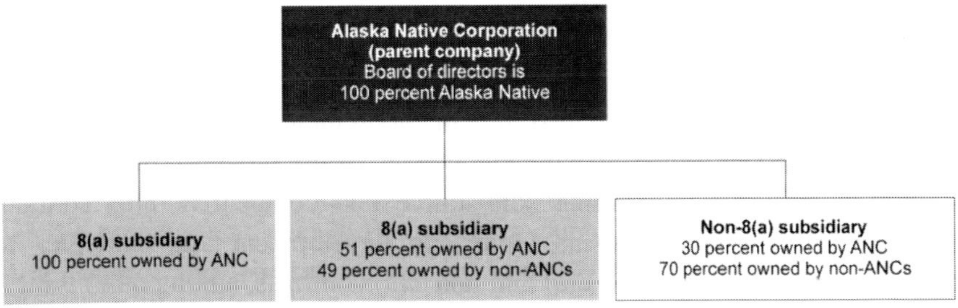

Source: GAO. | GAO-16-113.

Note: The example is an illustration and should not be viewed as generalizable to all ANC firms.

Figure 1. Illustrative Example of a Corporate Structure of an Alaska Native Corporation's (ANC) Family of Firms.

expected to verify, among other things, the proposed firm's size status to ensure that it still qualifies as small under the identified NAICS code.

Other federal agencies that would like to use SBA's authority to offer contracts to 8(a) ANC-owned firms also have an important role in the 8(a) process. For sole-source awards, these agencies can identify ANC- owned firms to whom they want to offer contracts and submit those offers to SBA for approval. In our prior work, agencies told us that the award of these contracts to ANC-owned firms provides a streamlined contracting process and assists agencies in meeting their disadvantaged small business contracting goals.[27]

2011 Revisions and Updates to SBA's 8(a) Regulations

In February 2011, SBA revised its regulations for the 8(a) Business Development program by adding language that (1) restricted the award of follow-on, sole-source 8(a) contracts to sister subsidiary firms owned by the same ANC; (2) made minor technical updates to outdated terminology regarding ANC ownership of multiple sister subsidiaries operating in the same primary line of business; and (3) revised existing rules related to ownership, compensation as a component of excessive withdrawals, and ANC-owned firm benefits reporting, among other things.[28]

The 2011 changes to the regulations include:[29]

- **Follow-on, Sole-Source Contracts-**Once an applicant is admitted to the 8(a) program, it may not receive an 8(a) sole-source contract that is a follow-on contract to an 8(a) contract that was performed immediately previously by another participant (or former participant) owned by the same ANC.
- **Sister Subsidiaries Sharing NAICS Codes-**Sister-subsidiaries of an ANC may not use the same NAICS codes for their primary lines of business.[30]
- **Other Reporting Requirements-**A number of clarifications and revisions were made to rules related to how compensation provided to firm officials impacts SBA's excessive withdrawal limits and the provision of an annual benefits report for ANC-owned firms. Specifically, SBA revised previous excessive withdrawal rules that, in SBA's opinion, unnecessarily hampered an 8(a) firm's ability to recruit and retain key employees or to pay fair wages to its officers. SBA, in its new rule, clarified that officers' salaries generally will not

be included within what constitutes a withdrawal unless, when looking at the totality of the circumstances, SBA believes the compensation represents an attempt to circumvent the excessive withdrawal limit. When SBA determines withdrawals are excessive and detrimental to the achievement of a firm's business development goals, SBA may initiate termination proceedings against a firm. Importantly, the excessive withdrawal analysis does not apply to withdrawals made by ANC-owned firms for the benefit of the ANC or the native or shareholder community. SBA also updated the rules for excessive withdrawals by increasing each maximum threshold amount by $100,000. Therefore, withdrawals are deemed excessive if in the aggregate during any fiscal year they exceed:

(i) $250,000 for firms with sales up to $1,000,000;
(ii) $300,000 for firms with sales between $1,000,000 and $2,000,000; and
(iii) $400,000 for firms with sales exceeding $2,000,000.

Finally, the rules also require ANC-owned firms to submit an annual report on the benefits distributed to ANC or the community.

WEAKNESSES IN SBA OVERSIGHT LIMIT ITS ABILITY TO ENFORCE PROHIBITIONS ON FOLLOW-ON, SOLE- SOURCE CONTRACTS TO ANC SISTER SUBSIDIARIES

As we have reported previously, SBA's ability to identify and enforce the regulations that prohibit the award of follow-on, sole-source contracts to subsidiaries of the same ANC is limited by a process that relies on the information provided by federal contracting departments and agencies, which we found in many cases to be incomplete.[31] According to SBA regulations, once an applicant is admitted to the 8(a) program, it may not receive an 8(a) sole-source contract that is also a follow-on contract to an 8(a) contract that was performed "immediately previously" by another participant (or former participant) firm owned by the same ANC. To assess whether contract awards are in line with this prohibition, SBA regulations require contracting agencies to provide an offer letter with details on 17 items related to the contract, such as type of contract, acquisition history (if any), contract value, and the names of any small business contractors who have performed the requirement in the previous 24 months.[32] Figure 3 below is an excerpt of the 8(a) program regulation outlining the items that must be included in an agency offer to SBA.

Required Items to be Included in Agency Procurement Offer Letters Submitted to the Small Business Administration (SBA) 8(a) Business Development Program

13 C.F.R. §124.502(c) How does an agency offer a procurement to SBA for award through the 8(a) Business Development program?

“(c) An offer letter must contain the following information:

(1) A description of the work to be performed;
(2) The estimated period of performance;
(3) The NAICS code that applies to the principal nature of the acquisition;
(4) The anticipated dollar value of the requirement, including options, if any;
(5) Any special restrictions or geographical limitations on the requirement;
(6) The location of the work to be performed for construction procurements;
(7) Any special capabilities or disciplines needed for contract performance;
(8) The type of contract to be awarded, such as firm fixed price cost reimbursement, or time and materials;
(9) The acquisition history, if any, of the requirement;
(10) The names and addresses of any small business contractors which have performed on this requirement during the previous 24 months;
(11) A statement that prior to the offer no solicitation for the specific acquisition has been issued as a small business set-aside, or as a small disadvantaged business set-aside if applicable, and that no other public communication (such as a notice in the Commerce Business Daily) has been made showing the procuring activity's clear intent to use any of these means of procurement;
(12) Identification of any specific Participant that the procuring activity contracting officer nominates for award of a sole source 8(a) contract, if appropriate, including a brief justification for the nomination, such as one of the following:
(i) The Participant, through its own efforts, marketed the requirement and caused it to be reserved for the 8(a) Business Development program or
(ii) The acquisition is a follow-on or renewal contract and the nominated concern is the incumbent;
(13) Bonding requirements, if applicable;
(14) Identification of all Participants which have expressed an interest in being considered for the acquisition;
(15) Identification of all SBA field offices which have requested that the requirement be awarded through the 8(a) Business Development program;
(16) A request, if appropriate, that a requirement whose estimated contract value is under the applicable competitive threshold be awarded as an 8(a) competitive contract; and
(17) Any other information that the procuring activity deems relevant or which SBA requests.”

Source: Code of Federal Regulations. | GAO-16-113

Figure 3. Excerpt from 13 C.F.R. § 124.502(c) on the 17 Required Items to Include in Offer Letters to SBA's 8(a) Program.

Senior SBA officials in Anchorage, Alaska, who oversaw about 50 percent of the active ANC firms in the program from fiscal year 2011 through fiscal year 2014 (the period of our analysis) —informed us that they enforce the regulation prohibiting the award of follow-on, sole-source contracts to ANC sister-subsidiaries exclusively by reviewing information provided in the procuring agency offer letters that agencies are required by program rules to submit.

According to SBA officials we spoke with, and as we found in our review of 30 large value sole-source contracts performed by 8(a) ANC-owned firms, an acquisition history and information on previous small business contractors was not always clearly provided by agencies in the offer letters for the contracts.[33] Two offer letters could not be located by SBA, as a result we reviewed a total of 28 offer letters. Our analysis found that 3 of 28 offer letters lacked any information about the contract's acquisition history, and 13 did not provide information on the firms that performed the work in the previous 2 years. However, if no acquisition history exists, regulations do not require that fact to be included in the offer letter. Likewise, regulations only require information on prior small business contractors that performed the work in the previous 2 years, and other types of firms need not be included in the offer letter. Table 2 outlines the extent to which the offer letters addressed critical information necessary for monitoring for follow-on, sole-source contracts.

Table 2. Extent to Which Critical Elements Were Included in a Non-Generalizable Selection of 30 Offer Letters from SBA and Procuring Agencies, 2011-2014

Information included in offer letter?	Yes	No Response[a]	Unclear[b]	Offer Letter Not Provided
Item 9: Acquisition history	17	3	8	2
Item 10: Names of the small businesses that previously performed the work in the last 2 years?	10	13	5	2

Source: GAO analysis of SBA and agency documents. | GAO-16-113

Note: For our analysis of 30 selected contracts, we were able to obtain 23 offer letters from SBA and another 5 letters from the procuring agencies. Neither SBA, nor the agency, was able to provide a letter for 2 contracts awarded through the 8(a) program, which we coded as "offer letter not provided."

[a] In some instances the agency did not provide a response to either Item 9, the acquisition history, if any, or Item 10, any small business contractors that performed the work during the previous 2 years. If no acquisition history or previous small business contractors exist, then no response is required under SBA's regulations.

[b] We found several cases where an agency indicated "N/A" in response to Item 9, acquisition history, but also listed a prior contractor in the offer letter. In one instance, an agency responded N/A to Item 9 and then did not provide any other information in its letter.

Outlining the acquisition histories and information about the small businesses that previously performed the work in the offer letters is critical to enforcing the prohibition. However, as our analysis shows, SBA did not regularly collect this information. SBA officials reported that they can send correspondence to procuring departments and agencies providing guidance on what information SBA needs to see when offer letters fall short of the requirements. In our review of SBA files for the 30 selected cases, we did not find documentation that SBA conducted any followed-up on nonresponses or instances where the responses provided were unclear in offer letters by agencies prior to our request. As highlighted in Table 2, we found 8 cases in which the agency indicated the previous acquisition history was not applicable; but then in the same offer listed a prior small business contractor that performed the work in the prior 2 years. In these cases, it is unclear whether the prior contractors listed actually performed the same work. In all examples where it is unclear, SBA cannot enforce its prohibition against sister-subsidiaries receiving follow-on, sole source contracts without following up with the agency to clarify its responses. When SBA does not have sufficient or accurate information in offer letters, and does not follow-up to obtain this information, the agency is not positioned to enforce its prohibition, as the agencies do not know whether or not a firm is a sister subsidiary of the prior small business contractor.

Additionally, we noted that SBA's guidance on offer letters did not ask specifically about whether the contract was a follow-on or not. Alaska District Office officials—those officials responsible for reviewing sole- source offer letters for 50 percent of the active ANC-owned firms in the program—agreed that it would be helpful if SBA required agencies to specifically list whether a contract is a follow-on, sole-source contract in their offer letter; as well as ensure that information about the incumbent firm, or the small business that previously performed the contract, that was awarded the previous contract, if there was one, is listed in their offer letter. According to these officials, they have found that the omission of this type of information in agency offer letters is sometimes due to the inexperience of or lack of understanding of key 8(a) regulatory requirements by procuring officials at other federal agencies, regarding what they should provide to SBA, and noted that the lack of guidance and training makes it difficult to fully meet program requirements. Senior officials in SBA's Office of Business Development, which has national oversight of the 8(a) program, also agreed that obtaining additional information in the procurement offer letters would be useful.

As a result of our site visit in October 2014, a senior Alaska District Office official developed a template to send to agencies providing guidance that specifically asks the agency to list whether a contract is a follow-on, sole-source contract in their procurement offer letters. The district office in Alaska provided us with one example of an agency using their template for an offer letter, which resulted in SBA obtaining the required information on acquisition history and whether the contract was a follow on. However, this positive change has not been adopted more broadly across the agency.

We have previously reported that information about follow-on contracts is not systematically collected or tracked by SBA or any other federal database or system. We recommended in 2006 and again in January 2012 that SBA reinforce to procuring agencies the requirement to provide the full acquisition history of the procurement in the offer letter, and direct district office business opportunity specialists to focus on this issue when they review offer letters for 8(a) firms. SBA neither agreed nor disagreed with this recommendation but did state in August 2013 that additional guidance regarding offer and acceptance will be fully delineated in the revised 8(a) Business Development program Standard Operating Procedures manual. As of October 2015, the guidance for SBA staff had not been revised.[34] Federal standards for internal control emphasize that guidance is a necessary part of an effective internal control system and should be periodically evaluated to ensure consistency and continued applicability to existing controls, such as regulations.

We also found that SBA did not maintain all required documentation in its files—such as offer letters, acceptance letters, and contracts—that would have allowed the agency to examine its previous records to independently determine whether contracts were follow-on, sole-source contracts.[35] In order to retain a delegation of SBA's contract execution and review functions, procuring agencies must report all 8(a) contract awards, modifications, and options to SBA. According to SBA's internal guidance, district offices must maintain files for all contracts awarded through the normal 8(a) review and approval process, to include all necessary contract documents. For contracts awarded through an SBA partnership agreement, the district office must maintain a copy of the offer document and notice of award, or first page of the contract, in the firm's business development file. Additionally, federal internal control standards require that agencies clearly document all transactions and other significant events, and all documentation and records should be properly managed and maintained.[36] When SBA does not maintain such documentation or take pro-active steps to collect this information when not provided by the procuring agencies, it is impaired in its ability to adequately monitor for follow-on, sole-source contracts. Table 3 summarizes the extent to which SBA was able to produce key documents that can help monitor for follow-on, sole-source contracts for 30 selected cases that exceeded the SAP.

As highlighted in Table 3, SBA was unable to provide us with the offer letters for 7 of the 30 contracts we reviewed, or 5 of 30 acceptance letters. Additionally, SBA could not provide us with 22 of the 30 contracts. For example, we found that SBA did not have any record of an offer letter or an acceptance letter on file for one physical distribution/logistics services contract valued at $337,000. Additionally, SBA officials reported that they were not aware of this contract until we brought it to their attention during the course of our review.[37] When SBA checked with the procuring agency, as a result of our inquiry, the agency supplied information about the contract in lieu of an offer letter. SBA noted that key documents were also missing for other selected contracts from this agency. SBA officials stated that this could be an indication that the agency procurement officer was not familiar with the terms of the partnership agreement and the requirements of the 8(a) award process.

SBA officials in the Alaska District Office and the Headquarters Office of Business Development stated that they face documentation challenges such as those described above in enforcing regulations prohibiting follow- on, sole-source contracts to ANC sister subsidiaries, and that more can be done by SBA to improve collecting data needed for this oversight. They also noted additional ways to improve SBA's enforcement of this regulation, such as providing additional training on this requirement to procurement agencies and additional guidance to SBA business opportunity specialists on how to respond to this missing information when determining whether to approve contracts.

Table 3. SBA Contract Documents Provided for 30 Selected Cases of Potential Follow-on, Sole Source Contracts, 2011-2014

	Document provided?	
Contract document	**Yes**	**No**
Procuring agency offer letter	23	7
SBA acceptance letter	25	5
Contract	8	22

Source: GAO analysis of federal procurement documents. | GAO-16-113

While SBA offers training to agencies on how to award sole contracts through the 8(a) program, the current training does not specifically address how to monitor for the prohibited type of follow-on, sole-source contracts. In 2006, we recommended that SBA improve its oversight practices by providing more training to agencies on the 8(a) program to specifically include segments that address ANC-owned participants.[38] In 2012, we further recommended that SBA reinforce the requirement for procuring agencies to provide the full acquisition history of the procurement in the offer letter and to direct district office business opportunity specialists to focus on this issue when they review offer letters for ANC-owned 8(a) firms.[39] SBA has taken some steps to address these deficiencies such as offering training that addresses this requirement.

In response to our draft report, SBA stated that—based in part on our discussions with agency officials during this review—it provided training to at least 19 different federal departments and agencies with over 1,070 contracting staff in attendance between fiscal year 2014 and 2015. SBA also reported that some of these sessions were recorded so that the information would be readily accessible for refresher courses as well as new hire training. However SBA did not develop similar training efforts for its own staff.

We continue to believe that there are opportunities to be more specific about what information needs to be obtained from procuring agencies because we found that the acquisition history and information on who performed the work previously is still not always being provided or sufficient enough for SBA to identify follow-on, sole-source contracts. In order to help improve this information collection, SBA could enhance its training to procuring agencies by specifically describing what the agencies should include in their offer letters regarding sole source contracts and the difficulty of enforcing the regulations without this information. Similarly, SBA business opportunity specialists could benefit from training that specifically addresses how to enforce this regulation, including what follow-up steps need to be taken when agencies do not provide adequate information and what to maintain in the files.

As we mention later in this report, SBA has yet to address problems with the guidance in this area. The guidance that is used by business opportunity specialists to administer 8(a) contracts is outdated—having been last updated in 2008, 3 years before the change in the regulations— and also does not address how to monitor for the prohibited type of follow-on, sole-source contracts. Ideally, when SBA updates its 8(a) guidance, it will include information about how a business opportunity specialist should collect information from agencies when offer letters do not include adequate detail. Federal internal control standards suggest that appropriate, policies and procedures exist with respect to an agency's activities. Without updated guidance in the form of policies and procedures that specifically address specific monitoring issues for the benefit of the business opportunity specialists, SBA will not be able to enforce this regulation.

We provide more detail on the implications of SBA's training efforts and its guidance for implementing the 8(a) program later in this report. Requesting that agencies specifically state whether a sole-source contract is also a follow-on in offer letters, providing additional training on this specific step to procuring agencies, as well as developing guidance to SBA officials on rules for collecting this data—would better position SBA to reduce potential violations of follow-on, sole-source contracting regulations, and to prevent the improper award of contracts.

SBA Faces Oversight Challenges in Detecting 8(a) ANC Sister Subsidiaries Operating in the Same Primary Line of Business, and Steps to Address these Challenges Are Still Being Formulated

SBA faces oversight challenges to detect ANC-owned subsidiaries owned by the same parent company from operating in the same primary line of business because of limited: (1) data collection and tracking and (2) information access and sharing across district offices, as we have previously reported. SBA has recently initiated steps to address these challenges, but these steps have not yet been completed.

Limited Data Collection and Tracking Poses Oversight Challenge for SBA, and the Agency's Steps to Address this Challenge are Incomplete

According to SBA officials, during enrollment and annual reviews, SBA enforces its prohibition on sister 8(a) ANC-firms having the same primary

NAICS code.[40] However, SBA's current systems still do not collect and track firms' underlying revenue activity as we recommended in 2006 and 2012, including revenues generated from secondary lines of business that would help SBA identify firms that are potentially circumventing the intent of its prohibition. Specifically, SBA 8(a) regulations prohibit an ANC from owning 51 percent or more of an 8(a) applicant that is the sister subsidiary of another 8(a) participant, which either at the time of application or within the previous 2 years, has been operating in the 8(a) program under the same primary NAICS code as the applicant. The prohibition's goal is to assist ANC-owned firms with diversifying their businesses in such a way that would enable them to survive in the market after they leave the 8(a) program. Program rules permit 8(a) firms to engage in secondary lines of work to promote their business growth. Thus, SBA's prohibition is intended to encourage 8(a) firms owned by the same ANC to expand their business activities by having them primarily engage in independent and viable businesses that perform separate and distinct work.

In general, SBA enforces its prohibition when ANC-owned firms initially enroll in the program and also during their annual reviews to ensure that the same primary NAICS code that a firm provides is not also being used by another sister firm owned by the same ANC.[41] For example, according to SBA officials, SBA's Division of Program Certification and Eligibility (DPCE) is required to verify that the primary NAICS code that an ANC- owned firm self-reports on its 8(a) application is not the same primary code used by a sister ANC-owned firm who is also participating in the 8(a) program. This office is also tasked with verifying that the primary NAICS code reported to SBA accurately represents the firm's business activities or intended business activities (in the case of newly organized concerns). SBA officials also told us that the San Francisco district office will also conduct this type of verification when a subsidiary submits a formal request to change its primary NAICS code. After SBA reviews an ANC-owned subsidiary's primary NAICS code during enrollment, SBA officials stated that district offices are to verify that the primary NAICS code that a subsidiary submits to SBA during its annual review is the same code that it reported during enrollment. However, beyond these checks, SBA does not currently have a regular or ongoing monitoring method or mechanisms in place for collecting and tracking firm activity, including revenues, to help ensure that 8(a) ANC subsidiaries owned by the same parent firm are not potentially circumventing the intent of SBA's prohibition as we have recommended in the past. Furthermore, under SBA's current regulations, after being certified to participate in the 8(a) program, there is no requirement that an 8(a) participant actually perform most, or any, work in the six digit NAICS code selected as its primary business classification in its application, and SBA may, but has not yet, revised its regulations to provide itself with the authority to unilaterally change a firm's primary NAICS code on its own. In fact, SBA permits 8(a) firms to engage in secondary lines of work to promote their business growth.

SBA's ability to track which NAICS codes are generating revenues for 8(a) ANC firms is limited and represents a long-standing vulnerability that we reported on before. For example, to help reduce this vulnerability, in April 2006, we recommended that the agency collect and track the revenues that subsidiaries generate under all their primary and secondary NAICS codes. However, SBA did not indicate whether or not it planned to implement this 2006 recommendation.[42] In January 2012, we then recommended that SBA develop a system to collect and track such revenue to help ensure that sister subsidiaries under the same parent company are not generating the majority of their revenue from the same primary industry.[43]

According to SBA officials, SBA attempted to design a database with the purpose of tracking firm activity collected by existing systems, including primary NAICS codes and revenues across the 8(a) program beginning in December 2011. However, in March 2015, SBA officials told us that SBA has decided to terminate this initiative because the database's design was not functional or compatible with existing SBA systems.[44] SBA officials told us that they were considering how their existing systems, including the Business Development Management Information System (BDMIS), can be improved to better support the agency's oversight efforts; however, they stated that they had no immediate plans or timelines for when this new initiative would begin or be finalized. As a result, SBA's existing systems, including BDMIS, still do not currently collect or track revenue amounts from primary or secondary NAICS code sources, limiting SBA's ability to help ensure that firms are complying with both the letter and intent of its prohibition. Fully implementing our 2012 recommendation would help SBA to effectively monitor all subsidiary activity and help ensure that such activity aligns with the goals of SBA's prohibition and 8(a) program.

SBA officials said that they are aware of some instances where ANC-owned 8(a) subsidiaries have potentially circumvented the intent of the agency's prohibition by entering the program under a primary NAICS code, but perform little to no work under that code. SBA has found that that these firms instead generate a greater portion of revenues in a secondary line of work under a NAICS code that another existing sister subsidiary uses as its primary NAICS code. According to SBA officials, this activity does not violate the agency's regulation because the prohibition only applies to the sister subsidiary's primary stated NAICS code, and not to the underlying actual revenue that an ANC-owned subsidiary generates in practice under other NAICS codes.

Because SBA does not require 8(a) firms to actually perform any work under their stated primary NAICS codes, there are opportunities for ANC-owned subsidiaries to circumvent the intent of this prohibition by generating a greater portion of revenues under a secondary NAICS code that a sister subsidiary is using as its primary code. For example, out of a non-generalizable selection of 39 parent ANCs we reviewed, we did not detect instances where parent ANCs actually violated SBA's prohibition by owning multiple 8(a) sister subsidiaries sharing the same primary line of business (expressed as a NAICS code). However, out of that same selection, we found that from fiscal year 2011 through fiscal year 2014, at least five ANCs owned multiple subsidiaries that generated less revenue under their primary NAICS codes than what they generated under a secondary NAICS code, which a sister subsidiary used as its primary code. Further, two of these five parent ANCs owned subsidiaries that generated no revenues under their primary NAICS codes from fiscal year 2011 through fiscal year 2014. If such activity is left untracked, a firm's secondary line of business could effectively become its primary revenue source in the same line of business that its sister firm claims for its primary line of business without actually violating the regulation. As mentioned earlier, we reported on this vulnerability in 2006 and 2012. Although this type of activity is not prohibited, as SBA has noted, it potentially conflicts with the intent of SBA regulations aimed at encouraging ANCs to ensure that their sister subsidiaries diversify their lines of business and operate independently. This is to ensure that the subsidiaries will be prepared to succeed as independent businesses in the open market after they leave the 8(a) program.

In one of the five examples, a parent ANC (ANC-30) owned two sister subsidiaries that concurrently participated in the 8(a) program from fiscal year 2008 through 2013, and both generated revenue under NAICS code 561210, as shown in Figure 4 below. However, Subsidiary 1 listed NAICS code 561210 as its secondary NAICS code while Subsidiary 2 listed this same NAICS code as its primary NAICS code. From fiscal year 2011 through 2014, Subsidiary 1 generated millions of dollars less in revenue under its primary NAICS code 334511 than what it generated under its secondary NAICS code 561210. (For illustrative purposes, see appendix III for five examples of ANCs that owned subsidiaries that generated millions of dollars in revenue in the same line of business as sister subsidiaries, while generating millions of dollars less or no revenue under their primary line of business. In this appendix, we do not illustrate all the ANCs that owned firms that participated in this same activity during the scope of our review.)

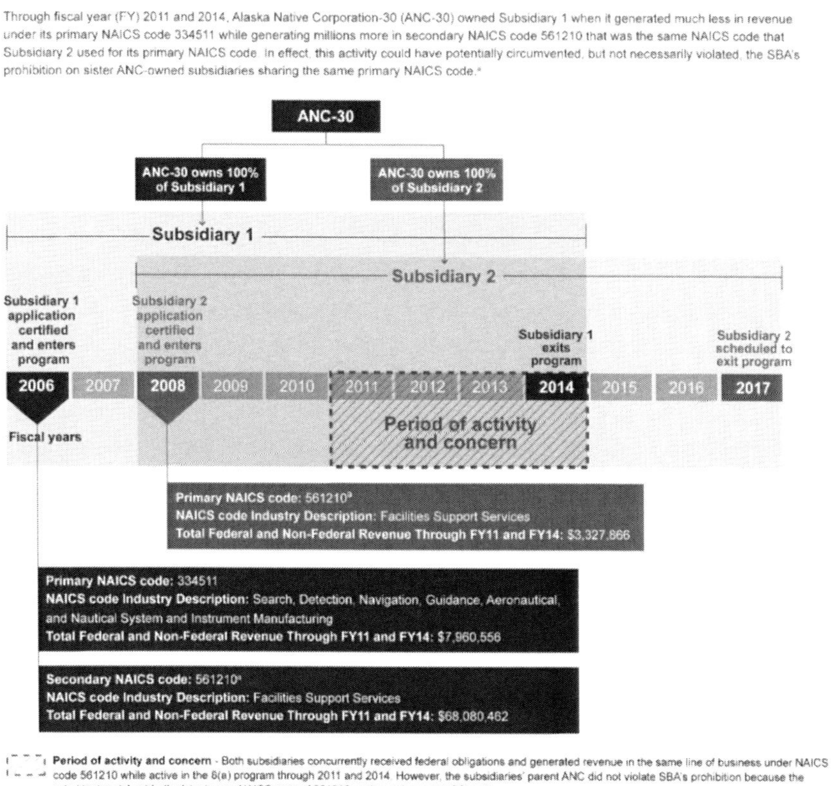

Source: GAO | GAO-16-113.

[a] SBA prohibits ANCs from owning 51 percent or more of an 8(a) applicant that is the sister subsidiary of another 8(a) participant which, either at the time of application or within the previous 2 years, has been operating in the 8(a) program under the same primary NAICS code as the applicant.

Figure 4. Example of Two Sister Subsidiaries Generating Millions of Dollars in Revenue in the Same Line of Business.

The firm activity we identified could be attributed to market conditions or business opportunities as ANC and SBA officials have noted, but, as we have previously reported, such activity warrants monitoring. According to one ANC official at an ANC parent corporation, when a subsidiary pursues work under multiple NAICS codes, the greatest portion of its revenue may naturally fall from its primary NAICS code to a secondary NAICS code from one year to the next due to market fluctuations or other valid business reasons that are unrelated to an intention to circumvent program rules. Likewise, SBA officials also told us that such behavior could be attributed to market occurrences as ANC subsidiaries seek 8(a) opportunities in diverse industries other than the industry for their primary NAICS code. We believe that this is one possible explanation for such behavior.

In February 2015, SBA proposed a rule that would effectively give it the authority to change a subsidiary's primary NAICS code when it finds that the "greatest portion" of the subsidiary's total revenues during a 3-year period have evolved from its primary NAICS code to a secondary NAICS code. According to SBA, this proposed rule will allow SBA to initiate a change of the relevant firm's primary NAICS code. If finalized as proposed, the rule would require SBA to give an affected firm the opportunity to provide any relevant information including revenues generated in the commercial market, documentation of the pursuit of contracting opportunities under the firm's primary line of business to establish that the firm's primary NAICS code should not be changed. The proposed rule was released for public comment in February 2015 and had not been finalized as of October 2015.[45] SBA officials indicate that the proposed rule may be finalized by mid-March 2016.

During the course of this audit, in June 2015, SBA officials told us that the agency had plans to take steps to further mitigate this potential vulnerability by using a random surveillance method to track and monitor the revenue generated under a subsidiary's primary and secondary NAICS codes. SBA planned to implement a random surveillance method by incorporating this method with its continuing eligibility reviews.[46] Specifically, according to officials, this method would involve using FPDS- NG data to randomly select ANC-owned subsidiaries that generate less or no revenue under their primary NAICS code while generating much more revenue in another NAICS code that a sister subsidiary is using for its primary NAICS code. This activity would have to occur over a period of 2 consecutive years. According to SBA officials, upon identifying such activity, the subsidiaries would have been notified about SBA's concern in writing during their continuing eligibility review, and asked to take precautions about engaging in this type of activity to avoid further action by the SBA.

Officials reported that they planned to start using the surveillance reviews by the end of September 2015. As of December 2015, SBA had not fully documented and implemented its random surveillance method.[47] However, in February 2016, after reviewing a draft of this report, SBA informed us that it had delayed plans for the random surveillance, and had taken steps in the interim to begin monitoring the revenue generated under a subsidiary's primary and secondary NAICS codes by tracking award obligations for all entity-owned firms in a spreadsheet.

SBA stated that this spreadsheet will be updated annually and its personnel will be provided instructions, consistent with a related proposed regulation, on how SBA associates should review the tracking mechanism. According to SBA, once the related regulations are finalized, the tracking system will be posted to SBA's intranet, making it accessible to all business opportunity specialists. However, in order to more accurately reflect firm activity in an industry, SBA would need to track revenues rather than just federal obligations, which may overstate or understate the amount of income actually generated.

Internal control standards state that agency procedures, techniques, and mechanisms to enforce management directives should be an integral part of an agency's planning and implementing efforts. As we have reported in the past, developing and using specific milestones and timelines to guide and gauge progress toward achieving an agency's desired results is a leading practice for effective strategic planning and management.[48] Documenting concrete timelines and milestones for implementing its random surveillance monitoring method, will better position SBA to effectively implement and operationalize its method for identifying firm activity that may circumvent, intentionally or not.

Limited Information Access and Sharing across District Offices Hinders SBA Oversight

Contributing to SBA's challenges in tracking NAICS revenues are limitations placed on SBA district office staff's ability to access and share important subsidiaries' NAICS codes across district offices. For example, SBA officials told us that their business opportunity specialists are responsible for overseeing 8(a) ANC-owned firms serviced across SBA's 68 district offices. At each of SBA's 68 district offices, the business opportunity specialists use the same internal database, including the BDMIS, to access and share subsidiary data for the ANC-owned firms that they are responsible for servicing—including the primary and secondary NAICS codes approved for use by the 8(a) participant. However, officials from SBA's Headquarters and four district offices told us that the agency's system rules and strict access privileges within these systems restrict business opportunity specialists from accessing and sharing NAICS code data across district offices. This includes NAICS code data for subsidiaries that their offices do not service, but are owned by the same parent ANC that owns subsidiaries that they do service. SBA officials told us that this access limitation can also occur within a district office when different business opportunity specialists are responsible for servicing different subsidiaries that are owned by the same parent ANC. SBA officials in headquarters told us that these access limitations are used to protect the privacy—the individual confidential business and financial information—of ANC subsidiaries.

Although we recognize privacy concerns as a legitimate reason for limiting access, federal internal control standards require that program data should be recorded and shared with staff in a form that enables them to carry out program controls and determine the extent to which compliance with various laws and regulations is occurring.[49] Our review indicates that such limitations can hinder business opportunity specialists' ability to systematically identify and examine relevant firm activity, including NAICS codes, of ANC-owned sister subsidiaries who are serviced by different district offices, and potentially circumventing the intent of SBA's prohibition.

In May 2015, SBA's Associate Administrator for the 8(a) program confirmed that limited information sharing across district offices creates vulnerabilities in program oversight. As a result, the Associate Administrator told us that the agency has plans to develop a more centralized and comprehensive oversight strategy. The new approach would give certain oversight staff the responsibility of accessing and monitoring relevant information for ANC-owned subsidiaries being serviced across different district offices, which would supplement the monitoring efforts of SBA's district offices.[50] This strategy would include monitoring for ANC compliance pertaining to all sister-subsidiaries being serviced across different district offices or business opportunity specialists. However, SBA officials told us that they do not have firm dates or specific plans for fully implementing this proposed monitoring strategy. Later in this report, we discuss what factors have affected the progress of implementing this strategy.

As the Associate Administrator develops plans to create, document, and implement the program's new centralized and comprehensive oversight strategy, officials have an opportunity to design an approach that upholds the privacy of information captured in the BDMIS database, while providing for the appropriate level of sharing and access to relevant subsidiary data, including NAICS code information, for tracking and monitoring purposes. However, it may be more effective and efficient for SBA to implement this oversight strategy after it implements our 2012 recommendation that SBA collect and track the underlying revenue activity generated under all NAICS codes.

As of October 2015, SBA does not have a database that collects and tracks the underlying revenue activity that firms generate in their primary and secondary NAICS codes, as we recommended SBA develop in 2012. As stated earlier, internal control standards state that agency procedures, and mechanisms to enforce management directives should be an integral part of an agency's planning and implementing efforts. The appropriate level of access to and sharing of relevant NAICS code data, including revenue data, will be an important control for SBA to include in its planning and implementation of the database that we recommended it develop in 2012, and its enforcement of its prohibition. Until SBA designs and implements such a database, the comprehensiveness of its oversight strategy, once implemented, will be limited to providing access to and sharing of NAICS codes themselves. It will not address the underlying revenue activity generated under those codes, which will give SBA limited assurance that the activities of sister firms align with intent of SBA's prohibition while the firms are serviced across different district offices.

8(a) ANC-Owned Firms Report Data on Distributed Benefits, Compensation and Revenues, but Missing Compensation Data May Limit the Alaska District Office's Oversight of the Firms It Services

8(a) ANC-owned firms self-report information on their benefits and compensation to SBA, but varying and missing information on compensation—including data used to determine whether withdrawals of funds from the company were appropriate—may limit SBA's efforts to assess compliance with related reporting requirements.

Most 8(a) ANC-owned Firms Selected Provided Information on Benefits and Revenues Distributed to the Community

Most of the 8(a) ANC-owned firms in our non-generalizable sample of 26 firms provided information on the benefits distributed to the ANC or the Native community.[51] In February 2011, SBA promulgated a rule requiring ANC-owned firms participating in the 8(a) program to annually report information on how they distributed benefits to their communities. Reports are to include information showing how 8(a) program participation has provided benefits to the native members or community, including information about funding cultural programs, employment assistance, jobs, scholarships, internships, subsistence activities, and other services.[52]

SBA's OIG reported in July 2009 that the revenues generated from the 8(a) program by 8(a) ANC-owned firms may be shared by hundreds, and sometimes even thousands of native shareholders unlike other 8(a) businesses—whose revenues generally go to one or two disadvantaged individuals.[53] SBA officials told us that one intended use of the benefit reports submitted by ANC-owned firms may be to respond to audits and congressional inquiries about the benefits of the 8(a) program. According to our analysis, 22 of the 26 ANC-owned firms in our non-generalizable sample submitted some form of benefits report between calendar years 2011 and 2014. Of the remaining 4 firms, 2 did not file any reports, and 2 other firms were either new entrants or completers of the program and were not required to submit any reports between 2011 and 2014. The Alaska Deputy District Director told us that SBA has not taken action against the 2 firms that did not submit any reports because the rules related to how the reports should be structured have yet to be finalized.[54] What has been submitted to SBA varied in terms of the detail provided in the report, ranging from a very general paragraph submitted by one ANC firm about distributions made over a 3-year period to a longer 13-page report submitted by another firm detailing specific benefits provided to the community. Formalizing the approach for the benefits report will be a good first step in collecting and utilizing these important data. See appendix III for an abridged example of a benefit report.

SBA also collects annual updates on the revenues made by ANC-owned firms participating in the program. As part of their submission, 8(a) ANC-owned firms provide information about the revenues associated with their participation in the 8(a) program as well as the non-8(a) federal contracts awarded over the program year.[55] Two of the district offices we spoke with indicated that they use this information to monitor the achievement of business activity targets starting in the program's fifth year. For the 4 years included in our review, these firms collectively accumulated slightly over $1.4 billion in 8(a) and non-8(a) revenues.[56] See app. IV for additional information on the revenues generated under the program.

Missing Information on Compensation May Make it Difficult for SBA to Identify Violations of Program Rules

Our review found that 8(a) ANC-owned firms serviced by the Alaska District Office—which represent 18 of the 26 8(a) ANC firms we reviewed—were allowed by the Alaska District office to provide varying levels of detail about compensation—including non-responses—in their annual updates despite the rules, which may make it difficult for this office to determine if firms have violated excessive withdrawal rules.[57] SBA regulations and the agency's 2008 program guidance call for firms to provide records of all payments, compensation, and distributions (including loans, advances, salaries and dividends) made by the firm to each of its owners, officers or directors or to any person or entity affiliated with any of those entities each year to their assigned SBA district office.[58]

We reviewed the compensation-related information for a non-generalizable sample of 26 8(a) ANC-owned firms required to submit this information to SBA. Of these, 10 firms consistently answered all questions in their annual updates related to compensation from calendar year 2011 through 2014.[59] By contrast, another 5 firms provided no details on compensation at the subsidiary level, but indicated in the reports submitted to SBA that the compensation was paid by the parent corporation. Another 7 firms were missing at least one year of compensation data. One firm that participated in the program between 2011 and 2013 did not provide any compensation data for those 3 years, and withdrew from the program in 2014. One firm entered the program in 2014 and a final firm exited the program in 2011. Thus, there were no reporting requirements for these two firms.

While we could not thoroughly examine whether all firms were complying with compensation-related regulations because of some limitations in the information that SBA collected, we were able to analyze a smaller number of firms that provided compensation data for all years in which they were program participants from our non-generalizable sample of 26 firms by their average annual sales between calendar years 2011 through 2014. Based on our review of the files provided, the overall compensation for firms' executives ranged from $0 to $820,793 annually as shown in Table 4.

Table 4. Annual Range of Executive Compensation for Nongeneralizable Selection of 26 Firms Reporting By All Calendar Years (2011-2014)

	2011	2012	2013	2014
Number of firms required to report compensation[a]	18	21	23	18
Actual number that submitted compensation information[b]	15	21	20	12
Compensation range	$18,987-	$0[d]-	$0[d] -	$0[d] -
	$820,793[c]	$365,846	$364,736	$267,851

Source: GAO analysis of annual updates submitted to SBA by ANC-owned firms. | GAO-16-113.

[a] As part of its annual updates provided to SBA, 8(a) firms are to include information on the compensation paid to certain employees each year. Annual compensation comprises all payments, compensation, and distributions (including loans, advances, salaries, and dividends) made by 8(a) participant to each of its owners, officers, or directors or to any person or entity affiliated with such individuals.

[b] Six firms indicated that their parent subsidiaries paid executive compensation and did not provide any compensation information. It should be noted that two firms in our sample—one firm that exited the program in 2011 and another that entered in 2014—were not required to and did not report any information from 2011 through 2014.

[c] The compensation reported for this firm includes salary, bonuses, and deferred compensation.

[d] While the salary for this executive was atypical, the firm's annual report did not provide any additional detail about the compensation agreement for this individual. It is possible that the compensation was deemed appropriate for this firm because it was in its first developmental year of the 9-year program and generated less than $500,000 in 8(a) revenues and $0 in non-8(a) revenues. Other key officials for this subsidiary received nominal compensation amounts ranging from $600-$900. We did note that this executive also worked for another subsidiary firm of the same parent ANC, where compensation may have been provided. This other subsidiary was outside the scope of our research

A key limitation of the data we reviewed was that not all firms provided compensation for all review years; in other instances we also noted that some firms did not provide any compensation to their executives, instead their parent corporation did. Our review also identified other differences that were reported about compensation to SBA from year to year for the same firms. For example, one ANC-owned firm in the construction industry provided compensation data for its president and chief executive officer for calendar years 2011 and 2013; but did not provide the same information in calendar years 2012 and 2014. Another ANC-owned subsidiary reported that its parent corporation paid the compensation for its officers for 2011 through 2013, but did not provide details on the compensation paid in those years. However, in its 2014 annual review, this same firm reported that its parent corporation compensated its general manager nearly $240,000. Another firm sent an e-mail to SBA in 2011 indicating that its parent corporation paid an executive's salary, and reported "not applicable" for compensation paid in 2013 and 2014. In this instance, SBA did not ask for an updated attestation from the firm each year as to who paid the executive's salary, and continued this firm's eligibility based on that 2011 e-mail.

The range in compensation is reflective of the complexity and diversity of ANC-owned firms. For example, according to three ANC association experts we interviewed, the compensation provided to officials and managers of ANC-owned firms is based on what the market will bear and similar to how compensation is set for other corporate firms. Additionally, according to these officials, compensation will vary according to the structure or development phase of the company and regardless of whether a manager is a native member or not. Because the size and structure of these subsidiary firms vary, we could not conduct comparisons within the group or to other firms in the private sector.

Although SBA requires compensation data on a firm's owners, officers, and directors annually, the Alaska district office did not collect this information consistently. For example, a senior official within the Alaska District Office told us that they do not collect this information because, based on their interpretation of the law, they believe 8(a) ANC-owned firms are exempt from providing this information. However, officials at district offices in Washington, D.C. and Richmond, Virginia—offices that service relatively fewer 8(a) ANC-owned firms than the Alaska district office—told us that non-responses are unacceptable under the rules of the program because non-responses are not allowed for other types of firms participating in the program. SBA has placed a statement on the forms that collect this information that there are no exceptions when reporting compensation data. SBA can build upon this initial step by outlining these same rules in program guidance. When these offices receive non-responses, officials at district offices in Washington, D.C. and Richmond, Virginia told us that they reportedly follow-up with firms regardless of whether a firm is owned by an ANC to obtain the missing information. Further, according to one senior district official in the Richmond District Office, the office takes additional steps to suspend any firms from receiving new contract awards until the required information is provided in line with their typical 8(a) practice.

As noted above, one 8(a) ANC-owned firm did not provide any information about compensation; however, the business opportunity specialist assigned to the firm took limited steps as part of the annual review process to collect this information. For example, the business opportunity specialist assigned to this review did not follow up with the firm to get the omitted information or take any adverse actions, such as recommending the initiation of termination proceedings for failure to provide the required information. Instead, the business opportunity specialist indicated in the review that the firm's continued participation in the program was deemed beneficial to the continued development of the firm. Program rules developed by SBA's headquarters indicate that all firms are expected to provide these data annually as a condition of continued program participation.

8(a) ANC-owned firms must also ensure that their officers' compensation does not circumvent SBA's excessive withdrawal limitations. As we discussed previously in this report, excessive withdrawals are defined under the 8(a) program as any cash dividends; distributions in excess of amounts needed to pay taxes; cash and property withdrawals; payments to immediate family members not employed by the participating firm; bonuses to officers; and investments on behalf of an owner.[60] However, the excessive withdrawal restrictions do not apply to ANC-owned firms where a withdrawal is made for the benefit of the ANC or the native or shareholder community. It does, however, apply to withdrawals from an ANC-owned firm that do not benefit the relevant entity or community, such as funds withdrawn for the benefit of a non-native manager or owner that exceed certain thresholds. Although officers' salaries are generally not considered withdrawals, SBA does count those salaries as withdrawals where it believes that a firm is attempting to circumvent the excessive withdrawal limitations through the payment of officers' salaries.[61] There are strict regulations limiting how much can be withdrawn from a firm for purposes other than benefiting the ANC or native or shareholder community, as SBA believes excessive withdrawals are contrary to the development of a fledgling business.[62] According to the guidance last issued by SBA in 2008, excessive withdrawals are to be calculated by SBA business opportunity specialists during annual reviews by reviewing 2 years of withdrawals, and the firm's sales data.

We found that district offices vary in their practices of applying the program's excessive withdrawal rules and their subsequent determination and calculation of such withdrawals. For example, according to one official at the Richmond, Virginia District Office, compliance staff cannot determine whether excessive withdrawals occurred without ANCs providing individual compensation worksheets to SBA. However, when determining whether excessive withdrawals took place, the Washington, D.C. District Office considers all information from a firm's consolidated financial statement instead. Finally, and unlike the other two district offices, as previously noted, the Alaska District Office accepts responses of "not applicable" or blanks on compensation data provided by ANC- owned firms making it difficult to consistently assess compliance with excessive withdrawal requirements.

According to senior officials in these offices, the variation in the practice of calculating excessive withdrawals is due to the lack of specific updated guidance on what financial information they are required to collect from ANC-owned firms since SBA's last guidance on this issue was issued in 2008 and there have been changes to the regulations since then. Without a consistent approach and updated guidance, the agency may not be aware when a firm has exceeded withdrawal limits or is using withdrawals in ways that differ from what is allowed under the regulations. SBA officials reported that they are currently developing program guidance, which is subject to agency clearance at the end of September 2015 and was scheduled to be finalized by December 31, 2015.[63] Thus, as this guidance was in draft at the time of our review, we were unable to assess the extent to which the updated guidance will clarify what financial information the district offices are required to collect from ANC-owned firms.

Weak Management Controls have Hindered SBA's Program Oversight

Weaknesses in SBA's data collection, supervisory review, staffing, and program guidance has contributed to weak program oversight and monitoring of ANC 8(a) firms. During the course of our review, SBA took a temporary step to address some of the deficiencies identified in our review and stated that it was planning longer-term actions to further strengthen controls.

SBA's Documentation of its Oversight of ANCs was Incomplete and Inconsistent

As discussed throughout this report, we found that incomplete or inconsistent documentation regarding ANC-owned firms limited SBA's oversight of the regulatory requirements we examined (i.e. the prohibitions against awarding sister subsidiaries follow-on, sole-source contracts; sharing of primary NAICS codes by sister subsidiaries; and annual reporting requirements for ANC-owned firms). The information SBA provided in response to our requests was sometimes incomplete and the level and type of required documentation obtained varied between district offices. For instance, SBA requires firms to submit updated information for annual reviews of their continued eligibility for the program. From the non-generalizable sample of 26 ANC-owned firms we used to analyze compensation and revenues, our review found that five firms did not submit at least one annual review during the time they participated in the program. SBA guidance requires SBA business opportunity specialist to enter this information electronically into the system that maintains annual reviews and other documents. When these documents are missing, SBA cannot be assured that the firm is continuing to meet its program goals or remains eligible for the program. Additionally, and as we noted previously in the report, SBA was only able to provide 23 of 30 agency offer letters for 8(a) contracts that we requested for our review of contracts that may have been follow-on, sole source contracts. When SBA does not properly maintain these documents, it is limited in its ability to enforce the prohibition against follow-on, sole-source contracts.

SBA also faced significant challenges in providing us with basic information on 8(a) ANC-owned firms, such as the total number of firms serviced by the agency. For example, it took 3 months for SBA to provide a list of ANC-owned firms in the 8(a) program, and on three separate occasions SBA officials provided three separate numbers for the total number of ANC 8(a) participants—ranging from 226 to 636. GAO's guidance on data reliability suggests that data should be accurate, valid, and complete.[64] Reliable data means that program data are reasonably complete and accurate, can be used for their intended purposes, and have not been subject to inappropriate alteration.[65] Additionally, federal internal control standards require that agencies maintain adequate documentation that clearly records all transactions or significant events, that these documents are readily available for inspection and review, and that it is useful to managers in their daily operations.[66]

Senior program officials we spoke with and a district office official in Alaska agreed that this was a program weakness and they need to better document 8(a) ANC-owned firm activities. Both a senior and district office officials in Alaska cited various reasons for the state of the files we requested for review, including frequent staff turnover. An Alaska district official also stated that a departing staff member did not record or save key contract and financial documents for an unknown number of ANC- owned firm files. SBA's inability to account for and make available principal information on all of the ANC-owned firms participating in the program raises concerns about the integrity of the agency's internal controls and ability to provide effective and sustained oversight. Unless SBA collects documents related to follow-on, sole-source contracts, benefits distributions, compensation data, the excessive withdrawals that do not benefit the ANC or the native or shareholder community, as well as the submission of the annual reviews themselves, SBA's ability to provide effective oversight of key program areas will be limited.

In response to a draft of this report, SBA stated and provided documentation that, in 2015, SBA staff in the Alaska District Office received detailed training on what SBA officials described as 8(a) critical procedures including file management, annual review processing, and related documentation. SBA also reported that its next steps are to continue ongoing training and mentoring in 2016 with monitoring of performance metrics and regular check-ins with the Office of Field Operations team by the Alaska District Office. SBA's actions to address the oversight staff's knowledge gap and limitations we identified in our review confirm that there was a need to improve the enforcement of oversight activities. The new briefings, training, mentoring, and follow-up monitoring are an important first step toward improving internal control in the Alaska District Office. However, it will not be clear whether these initial steps have resulted in more effective oversight of key program areas, until SBA can demonstrate that the agency is appropriately documenting ANC-owned firm files by providing documentation that is complete and accurate.

Inconsistent Supervisory Review of ANC Transactions and Related Documentation from Alaska District Office Increases SBA's Vulnerability to Potential Fraud

Our review of 26 ANC-owned firms' annual reviews files from the Alaska District Office showed that there was inadequate supervisory review for several of the annual reviews conducted by the business opportunity specialists overseeing these firms, and in some cases there was no appropriate segregation of duties for these reviews.[67] ANC-owned firms must submit annual reviews to their district offices documenting their progress over the program year.[68] Business opportunity specialists review the report and determine whether a firm has maintained its eligibility for the program. In our review of a non-generalizable sample of 26 sets of annual updates submitted to SBA by ANC-owned firms between 2011 and 2014, 10 annual reviews lacked appropriate supervisory review.[69]

Although SBA has policies for supervisory review of its annual reviews, which involve three levels of assessment before a determination of a firm's continued eligibility is finalized, it appears that the Alaska District Office did not consistently follow these procedures.[70] In 6 cases, the business opportunity specialist who initiated the review of the annual review also reviewed their own work. In these cases they also decided whether a firm could remain in the program. Federal internal control standards state that appropriate organizational structure and supervisory responsibilities that establish a separation of duties are integral components of effective oversight. Consistent with these standards, key duties and responsibilities, such as reviewing annual reports submitted by participating ANC-owned firms, need to be divided or segregated among different people to reduce the risk of error or fraud. No one individual should control all key aspects of a transaction or event. Without adhering to the supervisory review and separation of duties outlined in SBA's internal guidance, the agency limits its oversight of ANC-owned firms, and is more vulnerable to potential noncompliance of SBA regulations by the firms or SBA staff. Unless SBA takes steps to strengthen its enforcement of supervisory review practices at this particular district office and ensures that its duties are properly segregated and supervised, the agency will continue to be vulnerable to improperly executed annual review processes and may unknowingly allow potentially ineligible ANC-owned firms to stay in the program.

In response to a draft of report, SBA officials reported and provided documentation that SBA staff in the Alaska District office received detailed training on what SBA officials described as 8(a) critical procedures including secondary reviews and approvals, in 2015. SBA also reported that its next steps are to continue ongoing training and mentoring in 2016 with monitoring of performance metrics and regular check-ins with the Office of Field Operations team by the Alaska District Office. SBA's actions to address these limitations confirm that there was a need to improve the enforcement of this oversight activity. The new briefings, training, and mentoring are an important part of establishing the right internal control environment. However, until SBA can provide evidence over time that adequate separation of duties and supervisory review are consistently being implemented, we will not be able to determine whether these initial steps have resulted in more effective implementation of these key internal control process.

SBA's Alaska District Office Staffing Challenges Hinder Program Oversight

SBA officials reported that the frequent staff turnover has directly contributed to the limited number of staff in the Alaska District Office with ANC-owned firm expertise, limiting their ability to conduct effective oversight of the ANC program. As previously noted, the limited number of staff in the Alaska District Office has been a long-standing issue, and was also identified as a challenge during our site visit to that office in October 2014.[71] According to an SBA memo, and in line with our own site visit observations, because of the current staff levels in the Alaska District Office, supervisory review of contract monitoring activities and annual reviews fell behind, resulting in a backlog of oversight duties.

From 2012 to 2014, according to officials, staff attrition in the Alaska District office reduced the number of staff from five full-time business opportunity specialists generally overseeing about 60 firms each to 1 full- time and 1 part-time staff overseeing all the ANC-owned firms.[72] In addition to reviewing annual updates, according to Alaska district office officials, that district office can also expect to oversee hundreds of separate contract actions submitted by departments and agencies to the 8(a) and other programs in any given fiscal year, and is one of SBA's busiest offices for the program. SBA officials, external stakeholders, and both GAO and SBA's OIG have previously reported that the number of staff historically assigned to the Alaska

District Office were not adequate to address the demands for services needed from this office.[73]

According to a senior official at SBA and another in the Alaska District Office, in addition to the unusually high workloads assigned to each business opportunity specialist, the attrition in the Alaska District Office in recent years can be attributed to the agency undertaking Voluntary Early Retirement Authority (VERA) and Voluntary Separation Incentive program (VSIP) efforts.[74] According to an SBA official, the agency did not fully account for the impact of the VERA/VSIP on this district office, and therefore did not take steps to retain staff in offices already struggling with limited staff—such as the Alaska District Office. As a result, several officials reported that institutional knowledge greatly diminished at all levels of the 8(a) program and especially in the Alaska District Office, which contributed to challenges in performing SBA's oversight activities. The Deputy Associate Administrator for Field Operations told us that ideally the office would employ five staff based on the current caseload of ANC-owned firms in that district office, and each of these staff would be assigned no more than 100 or more firms. As of April 2015, the agency increased its staffing by two business opportunity specialists. However, two additional staff falls short of what a senior official at headquarters and an official at the district office consider to be the optimal staffing level for the Alaska District Office.[75]

Officials note that there are a few complications to hiring additional staff including the requirement for new business opportunity staff to have federal contracting skills, which is one of six areas with critical skill gaps that are in high demand government-wide; and the agency's current budget, which accommodates no more than three business opportunity specialists at this district office.[76] In its comments on our draft report, SBA stated that it has plans to hire another staff person in 2016 who will serve as an economic development specialist. However, based on our review of the supporting documentation that SBA submitted to us for this position, the economic development specialist's roles and responsibilities involve limited monitoring.

We have previously reported that to meet and address mission critical needs, agencies must not only determine the critical skills and competencies that will be needed to achieve current and future programmatic goals, which SBA officials reportedly have done; but they must also develop strategies that are tailored to address gaps in number, deployment and alignment of human capital approach for enabling and sustaining the contributions of all critical skills and competencies.[77]

Taking these steps, especially when facing fiscal constraints, is essential to agency's ability to address its needs. SBA was unable to produce any workforce planning report, even though SBA's OIG recommended that they perform a workforce analysis in 2008.[78] Until SBA develops a comprehensive approach to staffing its Alaska District Office, as previously recommended by the OIG, to include better workforce planning, such as managing attrition and retirements—it will likely continue to struggle with meeting the demands of its monitoring responsibilities.[79]

SBA Actions to Enhance Program Controls and Oversight not Guided by Documented Plans and Milestones

During the course of our review, SBA took some steps to address some of the deficiencies identified in our review, including taking short-term actions to immediately address short-comings in the Alaska District Office's oversight processes and longer-term steps to establish a continuing eligibility review unit and develop updated 8(a) guidance—but could not provide a firm plan or dates for the latter efforts.

Short-Term Actions to Address Deficiencies in the Alaska District Office

During the course of our review, SBA initiated some short-term actions that are intended to address some of the deficiencies identified in our review. For example, as a result of concerns expressed by 12 parent ANCs related to foregone contracting opportunities and delays in processing applications for entry by their subsidiaries into the program, one official told us that SBA conducted an accountability review of the Alaska District Office's oversight of ANC-owned firms in October 2014. According to this senior official, SBA found similar deficiencies to those we noted—including the lack of supervisory review, no appropriate segregation of duties, and inadequate staffing.[80] Senior officials began taking several actions to address the problems identified, including reassigning 150 8(a) files—including ANC-owned firms and others—to other district offices in SBA's Northwest Region for at least the next year and a half, reallocating the approximately 70 remaining 8(a) firms between the two business opportunity specialists in the Alaska District Office; and taking personnel actions including reassigning, retraining, and hiring new staff.

Table 5. Distribution of Reallocated 8(a) ANC-owned Firm Files by District Office

District office	Existing ANC-owned firm files	ANC-owned 8(a) firms reassigned from Alaska	Current totals for ANC 8(a) firm files maintained by district office
Anchorage, Alaska	199	(142)	**57**
Seattle, Wash.	4	87	**91**
Boise, Idaho	4	24	**28**
Denver, Colo.	2	9	**11**
Las Vegas, Nev.	1	14	**15**
Portland, Ore.	0	8	**8**
Totals	**210**	**142**	**210**

Source: GAO Analysis of SBA data. | GAO-16-113.

According to a senior SBA official, the reassignment of the files is a short-term solution intended only to redistribute some of the workload for a period of time, and is not intended to last more than 18 months. Table 5 outlines the redistribution of 8(a) files to other offices. One senior official indicated that the servicing of ANC-owned firms is best handled out of Alaska where the contracts with these firms are likely to be awarded and also originate. These efforts along with SBA's recent efforts to hire additional business opportunity specialists are a good first step towards addressing its needs and may provide short-term improvements. However, until SBA develops a longer term human capital strategy and addresses the internal control issues we identified these efforts will likely fall short of the sustained oversight that is needed.

Longer Term Actions Underway to Establish a Continuing Eligibility Review Unit

SBA has initiated some long-term actions to address its oversight challenges but lacks written plans and time frames for carrying them out. According to senior SBA officials, SBA planned to create a new continuing eligibility review unit in response to our previous recommendations to carry out duties outlined in the Business Opportunity Development Reform Act of 1988.[81] According to officials, beginning in 2014, SBA took steps to realign continued eligibility reviews as a separate and distinct function from the annual review process currently handled through the district offices. Although program officials reported taking some initial steps to establish a continuing eligibility review unit that will carry out these functions, such as conducting a number of trial run reviews in early fiscal year 2015, it lacks a final comprehensive written plan for systematically guiding the launch of this undertaking. According to the new Associate Administrator of Business Development, setting up a new continuing eligibility review unit is one of six priority areas to be addressed through recent changes in the office's leadership.[82] This official and other senior officials from Business Development told us that the continuing eligibility review unit will be designed to ensure better compliance with 8(a) rules by taking a more detailed look at the financial documents provided by ANC-owned firms and verifying the self-reported information supplied, among other things.[83] Also according to the new Associate Administrator for Business Development, this office will be designed to supplement the efforts of the district offices because the high-level annual reviews generally undertaken by the district offices have not been an adequate monitoring tool. However, SBA officials lack a comprehensive plan for managing the continuing eligibility review unit. When we asked SBA officials about specific details of their plans, they were not able to provide us with any firm dates or a written business plan. These officials said they could not share any documentation related to the practices they discussed because they are still under development.

According to the senior officials, the new continuing eligibility review unit has been fully staffed. However, the office lacks formal policies and procedures, and clearly defined roles and responsibilities to guide its activities. According to the officials, part of the delay in addressing these issues is due to change in leadership for the office and the appointment of the new Associate Administrator for the program. The officials also told us that while they continue to set up this office and begin its activities, they have trained staff in some of the district offices to undertake reviews of firm eligibility. According to officials, this office has conducted a number of reviews in fiscal years 2015 and 2016. However, SBA did not share detailed findings from these reviews. Federal internal control standards state that a critical part of establishing an effective control environment is to identify and define required tasks, and that the agency has written documentation such as policy and procedure manuals that describes these tasks. While SBA has taken some initial steps to establish a continuing eligibility review unit structured to conduct more thorough review of ANC's continued eligibility in the program, until the agency completely outlines and implements a plan for the functions and tasks the continuing eligibility review unit will undertake, including clarifying the associated time frames for establishing a fully-functioning office, potentially ineligible firms may continue to be enrolled in the program.

Actions to Finalize Program Guidance

SBA has not finalized its guidance that would address the 2011 regulatory changes related to ANC-owned sister-subsidiaries receiving follow-on, sole-source contracts, sister subsidiaries sharing primary NAICS codes, and excessive withdrawals. For example, SBA's existing guidance, which has been in effect since 2008, does not provide detail as to how business opportunity specialists are to specifically address whether a sole-source contract is a follow-on contract. Federal standards for internal control suggest that information should be recorded and widely communicated to management and others within agencies that need it, in a form and timeframe that enables them to carry out program controls and other responsibilities.[84] These standards also emphasize that guidance is a necessary part of an effective internal control system. Additionally, guidance is to be periodically evaluated to ensure consistency and continued applicability to existing controls, such as regulations. A senior official told us that SBA continues to develop this guidance and process the draft document through its internal clearances. However, the issuance date for the document has slipped repeatedly because of internal differences of opinion on what should be included and changes in leadership over the process, according to one senior official. Finally, in September 2015, an official reported that the document is scheduled for agency clearance at the end of September 2015 and was to be finalized by December 31, 2015. As our audit concluded, SBA did not make its scheduled target to issue its updated guidance in December 2015. Because of this, we cannot assess and discuss the extent to which it includes changes that reflect the 2011 regulatory updates, or whether the guidance is capable of providing a consistent approach to monitoring firms.

CONCLUSION

Federal agency obligations to ANC-owned firms participating in the 8(a) program represent a sizeable share of total obligations made to all firms participating in the program, with SBA contracts to 8(a) ANC-owned firms totaling about $4 billion and representing about a quarter of all 8(a) obligations made in fiscal year 2014. Given the magnitude of these obligations and because ANC-owned firms are exempt from some regulatory requirements in the 8(a) program, heightened attention is needed for firms participating in the program. Our prior reports on the program have detailed several long-standing deficiencies and many of these vulnerabilities and deficiencies still exist.

While SBA has taken some steps since 2011 to improve its oversight of ANC-owned firms in the 8(a) program, the agency's ability to enforce regulations that prohibit the award of follow-on, sole-source contracts to subsidiaries of the same ANC is limited by its reliance on incomplete information from contracting agencies. Obtaining complete data on follow- on, sole-source contracts, in addition to providing specific training and providing guidance to agencies on complying with the related policy, would improve SBA's internal controls related to this regulation and limit the potential to award these set-aside contracts to firms that are ineligible to receive them. SBA addressed some of the recommendations we previously made to strengthen their oversight. However, because limitations in SBA's processes for overseeing compliance with sole- source contract rules persist, additional actions would be beneficial.

Further, the goal of SBA's 8(a) program is to assist small businesses in developing self-sustaining operations that can graduate from the program and operate independently; therefore, SBA prohibits 8(a) ANC-owned sister subsidiaries from sharing the same primary NAICS code. However, limitations in SBA's internal controls, including the lack of consistent, ongoing reviews and tracking of NAICS codes and revenue data and limited access to relevant data for affiliated ANC subsidiaries that share the same NAICS code while being serviced across district offices, may be allowing some sister firms to primarily operate in the same line of business. The limitations could be mitigated by implementing recommendations we made in our 2012 report to effectively track NAICS revenue data, as well by taking additional steps to conduct regular reviews of NAICS revenue data. However, SBA officials also need to provide responsible staff with an appropriate level of access to the relevant data needed to more effectively monitor ANC subsidiaries. Although SBA has taken steps in the right direction by drafting a proposed rule that would provide the agency with the ability to change NAICS codes to industries where firms are actually receiving most of their revenue, without the proper tracking and visibility that we describe above, this rule will be difficult to implement effectively.

Overall, SBA has struggled to articulate and execute its oversight strategy over 5 years after updating its regulations. For instance, we found that its lack of updated program guidance on the 2011 regulations and limitations in information systems affected the agency's ability to execute proper oversight of internal controls for implementing the 8(a) program for ANC- owned firms. Moreover, without additional actions to (1) develop an effective and comprehensive internal control framework, such as ensuring that its Alaska District Office has complete and consistent documentation on firms in the program, (2) design policies to effectively enforce the separation of duties and supervisory or administrator approval when reviewing ANC-owned firms' progress and related documentation at this office, (3) approach staffing of its Alaska District Office in a comprehensive way; and (4) launch the proposed continuing eligibility review unit with the policies and procedures that include specific tasks and milestones, there is limited assurance that SBA can achieve the objectives of the program and at the same time maintain a high level of oversight and accountability to help ensure overall program integrity.

RECOMMENDATIONS FOR EXECUTIVE ACTION

To establish an effective compliance oversight process for ANC-owned firms in the SBA 8(a) program as part of SBA's efforts to develop a more comprehensive oversight strategy, we recommend that the Administrator of SBA direct District Office staff implementing the program to take the following three actions:

- Improve SBA's ability to prohibit follow-on, sole-source contracts from being awarded to ANC-owned sister subsidiaries participating in the program by (1) requesting that procuring agencies specifically state whether a contract is a follow-on in its offer letter, (2) providing additional training to SBA staff that specifically address how to monitor for follow-on, sole source contracts, and (3) providing additional guidance to SBA officials on the enforcement of related policies;
- Enhance internal controls and oversight of ANC-owned firms in the 8(a) program serviced in the Alaska District Office by enforcing policies regarding the separation of duties and supervisor or Administrator approval in order to improve supervisory review of ANC- owned firm transactions and related documentation; and
- Develop a comprehensive approach to staffing its Alaska District Office to include succession planning and managing attrition and retirements in order to improve the agency's capacity to keep pace with oversight activities.

We also recommend that the Administrator of SBA direct the Associate Administrator of Business Development to take the following three actions:

- Document its planned method for tracking revenue generated under subsidiaries' primary and secondary lines of business, with milestones and timelines for when and how the method will be implemented.
- Provide the appropriate level of access to and sharing of relevant subsidiary data across district offices, including primary and secondary NAICS codes and revenue data, once SBA develops a database with the capabilities of collecting and tracking this revenue data as we recommended in 2012.
- Enhance internal controls and oversight of ANC-owned firms in the 8(a) program by:
  - ensuring that all ANC-owned firm files contain all relevant documents in accordance with SBA program requirements to help facilitate SBA's review of compliance with applicable program regulations and guidance, including the collection of documents related to follow-on, sole-source contracts, benefits distributions reports, compensation data, information about excessive withdrawals that do not benefit the ANC or the native or shareholder community, as well as the submission of the annual reviews themselves; and
  - finalizing the agency's plans to fully launch a new continuing eligibility review unit, including identifying policies and procedures such as specific tasks, milestones, and timelines for the full launch of the office.

Agency Comments and Our Evaluation

We provided a draft of this report to SBA for review and comment. SBA concurred with two of our draft recommendations, reported that it has already taken action to implement two others, and did not concur two other recommendations. SBA also provided technical comments, which we incorporated in the report as appropriate.

In its written comments, SBA stated that its Office of Business Development has made significant strides within the last 8 months to close several of our recommendations from previous reports focused on the 8(a) Business Development program. SBA further stated that specific to this review of the 8(a) program, the agency has significant process improvements underway to address some of the recommendations in the report. SBA also reported that because of the audit's focus on data files prior to 2015 and earlier open discussions with us, many of the recommendations were anticipated and it believes are currently remediated by recent actions.

SBA reported that it believes that the agency has already effectively implemented changes to address our first recommendation that the agency improve its ability to prohibit follow-on, sole-source contracts from being awarded to ANC-owned sister subsidiaries participating in the program by (1) requesting that procuring agencies specifically state whether a contract is a follow-on in its offer letter, (2) providing additional training to SBA staff that specifically addresses how to monitor for follow- on, sole source contracts, and (3) providing additional guidance to SBA officials on the enforcement of related policies. SBA stated that it continually emphasized the requirement to provide contract acquisition history in its 8(a) Program partnership agreement training with the Federal Acquisition Community. In response to our review, SBA significantly increased training to other agencies in fiscal years 2014 and 2015 to specifically address this and other 8(a) program requirements. However, it did not develop similar training efforts for its own staff.

Although SBA reported that it has already taken steps to address our recommendation, the agency stated that it did not need to implement the first part of our recommendation to request that procuring agencies specifically state whether a contract is a follow-on in its offer letter because the FAR already requires this documentation. While both FAR § 19.804-2 and 13 C.F.R. § 124.502 suggest that procuring agencies should specifically state whether an 8(a) sole-source contract is a follow- on when the proposed contract recipient is the incumbent contractor, these provisions do not apply to a sister-subsidiary of the incumbent contractor. As we noted in our report, in order to monitor for violations to the prohibition of awarding follow-on contracts to sister subsidiaries of the same ANC, SBA officials instead rely on procurement histories that are, at times, missing or incomplete. Therefore, we believe that similarly requesting that a procuring agency offer letter always explicitly identify whether an 8(a) sole-source contract is a follow-on would help to improve SBA's oversight.

In response to the second part of our first recommendation, SBA stated that it did not need to increase training to its own staff because, according to SBA, it provided training to procuring agencies, consider the risk of follow-on, sole source contracts being awarded to 8(a) sister-subsidiaries of the same ANC to be low, and have practices in place, such as their random sampling surveillance reviews of contracts awarded through the 8(a) program, to address this risk. We believe that SBA's efforts to increase training to procuring agency officials is a positive step that should help to address our finding that these agencies did not consistently provide procurement history documentation. However, SBA's own staff reported that, not only was this information missing at times, but that they sometimes had difficulty determining whether a contract was a follow-on, sole-source contract when the acquisition history was provided. Further, as we describe in our report, these staff did not consistently follow-up with agencies when they could not make an informed determination. SBA subsequently stated in its agency comments that it provided training to its staff on all of the elements addressed in this recommendation. In reviewing the training documents, we found that only 1 of one the 12 training sessions that SBA provided referenced the prohibition against awarding follow-on, sole source contracts to sister subsidiaries. This training document did not discuss how to monitor firms for the prohibition, including: what documentation should be submitted, what information in the document to review, and what follow-up steps should be taken when the relevant information is not provided. In addition, SBA's current random sampling surveillance reviews of contracts awarded through the 8(a) program occur after a contract has been awarded and a potential violation has occurred. We do not believe that this practice represents a proactive approach to monitoring for follow-on, sole source contracts under the program. Lastly, we cannot conclude, as SBA did, that the likelihood of follow-on, sole source contracts being awarded under the program is low risk. While we did not find follow-on contracts in the 30 large value contracts that we reviewed, we did identify important weaknesses in SBA's ability to monitor these contracts for sole- source follow-on violations. Moreover, our sample of 30 contracts was not generalizable and represented less than 1 percent of all contracts. Therefore, we continue to recommend that SBA provide additional training to its own staff that specifically addresses how to monitor for follow-on, sole source contracts.

In response to the third part of our first recommendation, suggesting that SBA provide additional guidance to its staff, the agency reported that it provided additional training to its field staff officials on enforcing its related policies and is now holding back-to-back quarterly Field business opportunity specialist training sessions relating to all of our recommendation's elements. As we previously discussed, in our review of the training sessions, we found that it did not identify specific guidance on how to monitor for sole-source contracts. Moreover, as we note throughout our report, updating the outdated

2008 SBA standard operating procedure for the 8(a) program to provide official program guidance on this 2011 rule is necessary to fully address our recommendation on providing guidance.

In response to our recommendation that SBA enhance its internal controls and oversight of ANC-owned firms in the 8(a) program serviced in the Alaska District Office by enforcing policies regarding the separation of duties and supervisory review of ANC-owned firm transactions and related documentation, SBA stated that it did not concur because, according to the agency, effective measures are in place. Specifically, SBA stated that it arranged legal briefings, training, and mentoring for the staff in that office through 2016, that included secondary reviews/approvals, files management, and annual review processing. SBA's accountability review of that district office in 2014, which followed our site visit to that same office, resulted in similar findings. Specifically, the Alaska District Office did not always follow supervisory review procedures, the office lacked segregation of duties, and the files were not always properly maintained. SBA reported that its next steps are to continue ongoing training and mentoring in 2016 with monitoring of performance metrics and regular check-ins with the Office of Field Operations team by the Alaska District Office. SBA's actions to address the staff's oversight and implementation of internal controls are a positive step. However until these actions can demonstrate the elimination of the control weaknesses we identified, the recommendation remains valid.

SBA did not concur with our recommendation to develop a comprehensive approach to staffing its Alaska District Office, to include such actions as succession planning and attrition and retirement management in order to improve the agency's capacity to keep pace with its oversight activities. SBA stated that the agency already addressed and mitigated the potential for reoccurrence of staffing issues through recent new hires and training. The agency acknowledged previous customer service challenges and inadequate staffing due to attrition in the Alaska District Office in recent years. The agency noted, however, that it recently hired two business opportunity specialists in 2015, with another business opportunity specialist and economic development specialist hire pending by February 2016. Along with the increased staffing, to address the knowledge gap regarding ANC 8(a) programs and procedures for all Alaska District Office staff, the agency reported that it provided 10 legal and ANC 8(a) training sessions to Alaska District Office staff. SBA also referenced its response to GAO-15-347 as support for its succession planning efforts. In that recent report we recommended that SBA improve the agency's human capital management by completing a workforce plan that includes key principles such as a competency and skill gap assessment and long-term strategies to address its skill imbalances. SBA agreed with that recommendation and responded by stating that a workforce plan was under development. However, SBA officials were not able to provide this workforce plan to us for this review or demonstrate how it related to the succession planning needs we identified in the Alaska District Office. Given that we have reported on inadequate staffing for overseeing ANCs in the 8(a) program in this particular district office since 2006, we believe that our recommendation to develop a comprehensive approach to staffing its Alaska District Office, to include such actions as succession planning and attrition and retirement management is still needed.

In response to our two recommendations that (1) SBA document its plans for tracking revenues generated under subsidiaries' primary and secondary lines of business and (2) provide the appropriate level of access to and sharing of subsidiary data across district offices, SBA concurred with these recommendations and indicated it had recently established a new tracking system that analyzed the obligations reflected in FPDS-NG for all entity-owned firms. According to SBA, as an interim step to developing a random surveillance method, it has begun monitoring the revenue generated under a subsidiary's primary and secondary NAICS codes by tracking award obligations for all entity-owned firms in a spreadsheet. SBA stated that this spreadsheet will be updated annually and its personnel will be provided instructions, consistent with a related proposed regulation, on how SBA associates should review the tracking mechanism. Once the related regulations are finalized, SBA plans to make it accessible to all business opportunity specialists via the agency's intranet. SBA's effort to track the obligations generated by firms in their primary and secondary NAICs codes is a good first step. However, in order to more accurately reflect a firm's activity in an industry, SBA should track revenues, as we recommended, rather than just federal obligations, since federal obligations may overstate or understate the amount of income actually generated. Additionally, SBA stated that it believes it has addressed our recommendations in terms of milestones and timelines, given that the new spreadsheet will be updated annually. However, given the level of effort involved in getting data from all of these firms, any method used to report these data requires planning and coordination that would be best achieved by developing written plans, with timelines and milestones. SBA's plans to share the spreadsheet used to track firm's obligations among all business opportunity specialists will address our fifth recommendation, once this information includes data about the firm's primary and secondary revenue streams.

Finally, we recommended that SBA enhance its internal controls and oversight of ANC-owned firms in the 8(a) program by ensuring that all ANC-owned firm files contain all relevant documents in accordance with SBA program requirements and finalizing the agency's plans to launch its new certification and ongoing eligibility office, including identifying policies and procedures such as specific tasks, milestones, and timelines for the full launch of the office. SBA reported that it has recently addressed this recommendation through the briefing, training, mentoring, and follow-up performance reviews that were previously mentioned and by setting up the Office of Certification and Eligibility. While these efforts are positive initial steps toward implementing our recommendation, it remains to be seen whether SBA's recent efforts will eliminate the control weaknesses we identified. With regard to the management of its files, SBA needs to ensure that its approach to briefings, training, and mentoring are sustained beyond this initial roll out and it needs to demonstrate that the procedures the mentoring team identified are implemented effectively. SBA also indicated that the Office of Certification and Eligibility is fully staffed and has conducted a number of eligibility reviews. However, SBA was unable to provide documentation of this office's policies, procedures, and milestones for conducting such reviews, which are necessary to provide a consistent and sustained approach to the reviews moving forward. Therefore, until SBA has fully developed and documented these internal controls, we continue to believe that our recommendation is needed.

Seto J. Bagdoyan
Director, Forensic Audits and Investigative Service

APPENDIX I: OBJECTIVES, SCOPE AND METHODOLOGY

The objectives of this review were to examine the extent to which: (1) SBA enforces its regulations prohibiting the award of follow-on, sole- source 8(a) contracts to subsidiaries of the same ANC; (2) SBA limits subsidiaries of the same ANC from operating in the same primary line of business; (3) information is known about compensation, revenues, and benefits distribution of ANC-owned firms; and (4) SBA has addressed challenges, if any, to its oversight and monitoring of ANC-owned firm participating in the 8(a) program since 2011.[85] This report exclusively discusses these issues in the context of ANC-owned firms participating in the 8(a) program.

Table 6. Characteristics of Case File Selections for Certain ANC-owned firms participating in the 8(a) program, 2011-2014

Research Objective	Purpose of Review	Number selected for review	How selected
Objective 1: To determine the extent to which SBA enforces its regulations prohibiting the award of follow-on, sole- source 8(a) contracts to subsidiaries of the same ANC	Possible sole-source, follow on contracts	30	Randomly selected from 155 contracts awarded to ANC-owned firms from 2011 through 2014 that met criteria for possible follow-on characteristics and were not small- value contracts.
Objective 2: To determine the extent to which SBA limits subsidiaries of the same ANC from operating in the same primary line of business	Monitoring NAICS codes	39	All ANCs where a unique parent ANC owned subsidiaries that earned at least $1 in 8(a) contracts from 2011 through 2014.
Objective 3: To determine the extent to which information is known about compensation, revenues, and benefits distribution of ANC-owned firms	Compensation and Revenue	26	Randomly selected 30 firms from all firms participating in the program from 2011 through 2014 that appeared to be ANC-owned, according to FPDS-NG. Four of these firms were found to be out of scope upon review, because they were not actually ANC-owned.

Source: GAO analysis. Note: We did not select any cases for review for our 4th research objective.

For the data analyses completed for all four objectives, we reviewed 8(a) program data on ANC-owned firms participating in the program from fiscal year 2011 through fiscal year 2014 to reflect the effective date of regulations included in our scope and to use the most recent data available. To perform our work, we used the Federal Procurement Database System–Next Generation (FPDS-NG) to select three sets of non-generalizable case selections or samples with 8(a) ANC-owned firms that met specific criteria for three of our four objectives.[86] Table 6 summarizes characteristics for each of our case selections. For each of these three objectives, we selected a subset of cases for follow-up review and illustrative examples, and therefore our findings are not generalizable to the entire population of ANC-owned firms participating in the 8(a) program. These selections are described in more detail below.

DATA RELIABILITY

During the course of our review, we identified data limitations with our primary data source—FPDS-NG, such as: miscoded 8(a) firms and incorrect obligations. To mitigate these limitations, we interviewed knowledgeable individuals about the data and corrected errors we identified. To ensure that we only completed reviews for 8(a) firms within the scope of our analysis, we interviewed agency officials who could provide more detail about the firms we selected. For objective 2, specifically, we held several interviews with ANC parent corporations and some 8(a) ANC-owned firms to corroborate revenue data for fiscal years 2011 through 2014. With executives and staff from the ANC parent corporations, we discussed data quality controls, validation techniques, metrics reporting, and oversight. We also assessed the reliability of our data by reviewing agency policies and internal controls, Office of Inspector General reports, and related documentation. Additionally, we took steps to verify the accuracy of the data, including performing electronic testing to identify missing data, outliers, and errors. Additionally, we traced randomized sample lists to the source data to ensure the validity of internally created files. We tested the reliability of the data we obtained from the other systems used to support this objective—Dynamic Small Business Search (DSBS) system and System for Award Management (SAM) by interviewing cognizant officials at SBA and corroborating data with ANC-owned firms.[87] We determined that the data from all systems were sufficiently reliable for the purpose of identifying contracts with characteristics that we wished to review for our research objectives.

FOLLOW-ON, SOLE- SOURCE CONTRACTS

To identify the extent to which SBA enforces its regulations prohibiting the award of follow-on, sole-source 8(a) contracts to subsidiaries of the same ANC, we assessed the agency's policies and procedures related to this control, conducted analysis of offering letters, contracts and other materials, reviewed a non-generalizable selection of contracts that met certain criteria (described below), and interviewed cognizant staff. Because there is no federal database that identifies follow-on, sole- source contracts, we used several variables contained within FPDS-NG as proxies for identifying potential instances of 8(a) follow-on, sole-source awards to ANC subsidiaries, such as company name, location, product or service, and contract award dates to firms and sister subsidiaries. Using these proxies as our criteria, we identified as many as 155 contract actions that had the potential to be follow-on, sole-source contracts. We randomly selected 53 contract files by identifying contract actions between 2011 and 2014 that had the potential to be follow-on, sole- source contracts. Of these 53 contracts:

- 23 had values of $150,000 or less. We removed these 23 contracts from any additional review because these agencies with small value contracts were not required to provide SBA with offer letters. Because SBA previously delegated contract execution authority to the procuring agency, procuring agencies could award these contracts without having to notify SBA first. Because no notification was needed in these instances, SBA would not have been able to determine whether offers were follow-on, sole source contracts until after the award had been made. Further, SBA officials reported to us that such contracts are less likely to be follow-ons because of their limited scope and duration.
- To review the remaining 30 large value contract actions, we asked SBA to supply relevant documentation about all contract actions.[88] We took additional steps to corroborate what we learned from SBA or to provide additional detail where needed. Specifically, we met with 10 federal departments and agencies that awarded these contracts between 2011 and 2014. We interviewed procuring agency staff using

semi-structured interviews and asked staff at these agencies to provide additional information (i.e. contract documentation including missing agency offer letters, SBA acceptance letters, contracts, and modifications for each possible incumbent and follow-on contract pair) we were unable to obtain from SBA. The results of our analysis are not generalizable to the entire population of ANCs participating in the 8(a) program, and we are unable to determine whether there could be other follow-on, sole-source contracts that our methods did not identify.

MONITORING NAICS CODES

To evaluate the extent to which SBA limits subsidiaries of the same ANC from operating in the same primary line of business, we reviewed SBA policies, guidance, and procedures in place at the time of our audit. We also analyzed ANC subsidiary data from three publically-available data systems: FPDS-NG, SAM, and DSBS system.[89] We selected from FPDS- NG, all contracts where there was a unique parent ANC with each owning multiple subsidiaries active in the 8(a) program from fiscal year 2011 through 2014, and where each subsidiary of that parent generated at least $1 in 8(a) contract obligations over this time period. There were a total of 39 ANCs that met these criteria.[90] We selected this timeframe because in February 2011 SBA made technical updates to regulatory language in SBA's regulation prohibiting ANC subsidiaries sharing the same primary North American Industry Classification System (NAICS) code.[91] This timeframe was also consistent with the timeframe used in other sections of this report. Our findings under this objective are not generalizable to the entire population of ANCs participating in the 8(a) program, although they do represent all contracts where these criteria were met by analyzing the FPDS-NG data.

We used SAM and DSBS to identify and analyze the dates that our select ANC subsidiaries entered and exited the 8(a) program. We also used SAM and DSBS to identify and analyze the subsidiaries primary and secondary NAICS codes used during the 8(a) program.

To corroborate the summary data we obtained from FPDS-NG, SAM, and DSBS, we requested certain documentary evidence from SBA, including subsidiaries' 8(a) applications and annual reviews. The summary data included subsidiaries' federal obligation amounts, primary and secondary NAICS codes used, and the 8(a) program entrance and exit dates. However, SBA was unable to provide all the documents requested within our audit timeframes. As a result, we contacted our selected ANCs to verify the subsidiary data we obtained from these three data systems. We used semi-structured questions to interview personnel from the ANCs and subsidiaries. During these interviews, we asked specific questions about the ANC subsidiaries' experiences participating in the 8(a) program. Additionally, we also requested the ANCs to verify summary data we collected from SAM, DSBS, and FPDS-NG. We also requested that the ANCs provide the total revenue amounts that the select ANC subsidiaries earned from fiscal year 2011 through fiscal year 2014. One ANC chose not to provide this revenue data.

Some of the summary data we collected from FPDS-NG, DSBS, and SAM were not always consistent with data provided by SBA or the ANCs, and we note these inconsistencies in our report. Nonetheless, we determined that the summary data obtained from the three data systems were sufficiently reliable for our purposes, except where noted in our report.

Compensation, Revenues and Benefits Distribution

To determine what information is reported to SBA regarding the compensation, revenues, and benefits distribution of ANC-owned firms, we reviewed ANC-owned firm 8(a) applications and annual updates. We also reviewed data on ANC subsidiaries active from fiscal year 2011 through fiscal year 2014 based on a non-generalizeable sample of 30 randomly selected ANC subsidiaries from FPDS-NG. Much of the data that we reviewed was self-reported by ANC-owned subsidiaries and could not be corroborated with other sources. To provide context the data we analyzed, in addition to speaking with officials from SBA, we also conducted interviews with officials from three associations that represent the interests of the chief executive officers of the 12 Native Regional Corporations, issues related to Native federal contracting, and indigenous people generally about their knowledge of compensation paid by ANC- owned firms. From FPDS-NG, we selected a non-generalizable sample of 30 unique ANC-owned firms active in the program between 2011 and 2014. We removed 4 of these firms because we ultimately found that they were not ANC-owned firms, and thus we reviewed data from 26 subsidiaries. Descriptive characteristics, including information about ANC ownership of the 26 ANC-owned firms in our non-generalizable sample is outlined in app. II and IV. Our findings under this objective are not generalizable to the entire population of ANC-owned firms participating in the 8(a) program.

ASSESSING MANAGEMENT CONTROLS

To assess the extent to which SBA has addressed challenges, if any, to its oversight and monitoring of ANC-owned firm participating in the 8(a) program since 2011, we reviewed SBA's implementation of program mechanisms used to ensure the compliance of regulations related to our scope of work. We reviewed relevant SBA controls, policies, procedures, and guidance, and assessed the extent to which these mechanisms effectively aligned with federal standards for internal controls.[92] Additionally, we selected four offices to interview officials about their practices. Two of the three offices we visited in person. All four offices were selected because of the role they play in the 8(a) program—such as certifying initial applications for the program, which is the responsibility of the San Francisco office; or, for the number of ANC 8(a) firms they service. For example, we selected a District office that served a large number of ANC firms (e.g. the Alaska District Office) and ones that served a smaller number of firms (e.g. Washington, D.C., and Richmond, Virginia district offices) to compare their practices. We conducted site visits to both the Anchorage, Alaska, and Washington, D.C. district offices. During these site visits, we interviewed staff and made attempts to conduct file reviews of selected ANC subsidiaries serviced by those district offices. We held a few semi-structured interviews designed to document SBA's practices and policies with regard to monitoring for follow-on, sole-source contracts, and sharing of NAICS codes. We also discussed with officials procedures for reviewing program application and annual reviews submitted by ANC-owned firms. Specifically with regard to the annual reviews, we discussed with officials what information is collected for ownership, compensation, excessive withdrawals, benefits reporting and revenues. As a part of our site visit to SBA's district office in Anchorage, Alaska, we collected data related to SBA's human capital planning for that office. Our methods for this specific part of the engagement included reviewing documentary evidence and interviewing cognizant officials with expertise in workforce planning methods. During these interviews, we discussed workforce plans, historical and current staffing numbers, and challenges. We asked about the skills and competencies needed to achieve program results, discussed the agency's strategies to address staffing gaps, and building necessary capacity. Additionally, we reviewed our own past work on human capital issues for guidance.[93] To inform other aspects of this objective, and to learn about proposed changes to SBA's existing regulations, especially those affecting the use of NAICS codes, we attended an SBA tribal consultation in Anchorage, Alaska. While we were in Anchorage, Alaska, we also met and attempted to meet with officials from a number of ANC- owned firms and one ANC advocacy group to obtain the overall perspectives of ANCs and their subsidiary firms on the 2011 regulatory changes to the program.

We conducted this performance audit from May 2014 to January 2016 in accordance with generally accepted government auditing standards. Those standards require that we plan and perform the audit to obtain sufficient, appropriate evidence to provide a reasonable basis for our findings and conclusions based on our audit objectives. We believe that the evidence obtained provides a reasonable basis for our findings and conclusions based on our audit objectives.

APPENDIX II: OWNERSHIP CHARACTERISTICS OF 26 8(A) ALASKA NATIVE CORPORATION (ANC)-OWNED FIRMS

The 8(a) ANC-owned firms that we selected for review were primarily wholly owned subsidiaries that reported few changes in ownership or management control over our period of study, as illustrated in Table 6 below. Most subsidiaries were previous or current participants in the 8(a) program. Of the 26 8(a) ANC-owned firms selected for our file review, 21 were wholly owned by an ANC parent corporation. Five firms were partially owned by an ANC that held the majority of ownership in the subsidiary and a few firms were partnerships with non-disadvantaged individuals who controlled a minority interest in the firm.

The 26 ANC-owned firms we reviewed were almost always part of a larger family of firms. In all, there were 243 subsidiary firms affiliated with the 26 8(a) ANC-owned firms selected as part of our review. Of these 243 subsidiary firms, 149 of them participated at some point in the 8(a) program. Table 7 provides additional detail about the ownership of ANC subsidiary firms in our sample. These characteristics are not generalizable to all ANC-owned firms.

Table 7. Ownership Details for 26 Selected Alaska Native Corporation-owned Firms, 2011-2014

	Percent of Firm Owned by ANC	Number of Sister Subsidiaries in Family of Firms	Number of Sister Subsidiaries that were Former/Current Participants in 8(a)	Change in Ownership
Corporations and Limited Liability Corporations (n-21)				
Firm 1	100	13	9	No
Firm 2	100	—[a]	—[a]	No
Firm 3	100	6	2	No
Firm 4	100	6	6	No
Firm 5	100	7	7	No
Firm 6	100	15	11	No
Firm 7	100	40	19	No
Firm 8	100	5	4	No
Firm 9	100	18	18	No
Firm 10	100	—[a]	—[a]	No
Firm 11	100	2	2	No
Firm 12	100	—[a]	—[a]	No
Firm 13	100	4	3	No
Firm 14	100	—[a]	—[a]	No
Firm 15	100	7	6	No
Firm 16	100	24	5	No
Firm 17	100	—[a]	—[a]	No
Firm 18	100	11	10	No
Firm 19	100	13	11	Yes
Firm 20	100	12	6	No
Firm 21	100	—[a]	—[a]	No
Partnerships (n=5)				
Firm 22	96	40	14	Yes
Firm 23	51	9	6	No
Firm 24	51	—[a]	—[a]	No
Firm 25	88	2	2	Yes
Firm 26	51	9	8	No

Source: GAO analysis of ANC-owned firm annual reviews and application materials.

[a] These firms share a common parent ANC. We have removed the corresponding data to avoid over counting.

APPENDIX III: 5 ILLUSTRATIVE EXAMPLES OF ALASKA NATIVE CORPORATIONS (ANC)-OWNED FIRMS AND THEIR USE OF NAICS CODE IN THE 8(A) PROGRAM, FISCAL YEARS 2011-2014

In our review of 39 ANCs, we found 5 ANCs, from fiscal year 2011 through 2014, that fully owned 8(a) subsidiaries that concurrently generated millions in a common NAICS code used by a sister subsidiary as a primary NAICS code, while generating less or no revenue under their own primary NAICS code. If such activity is left untracked, one firm's secondary line of business could effectively become its primary revenue source in the same line of business that a sister firm claims for its primary line of business without actually violating SBA's prohibition. Such activity could, intentionally or not, potentially circumvent the intent of SBA's prohibition on sister subsidiaries sharing the same primary NAICS code. This is a long-standing risk that we reported on in 2006 and 2012.

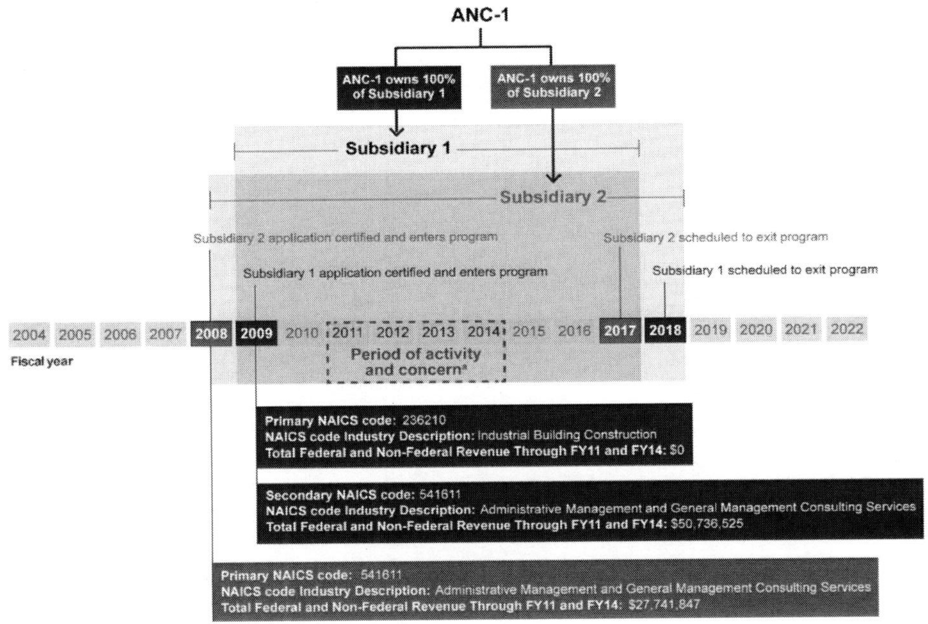

Source: GAO. | GAO-16-113

[a] Period of activity and concern: Through FY 2011 and FY 2014, ANC-1 fully owned Subsidiary-1 and Subsidiary 2. During this timeframe, Subsidiary-1 generated no revenue under its primary NAICS code 236210; however, it generated millions under secondary NAICS code 541611, which was the same code used for Subsidiary-2's primary NAICS code.

Figure 5. Illustrative Example of Alaska Native Corporations (ANC)-owned Firms and their Use of NAICS Code in the 8(a) Program, Fiscal Years 2011-2014.

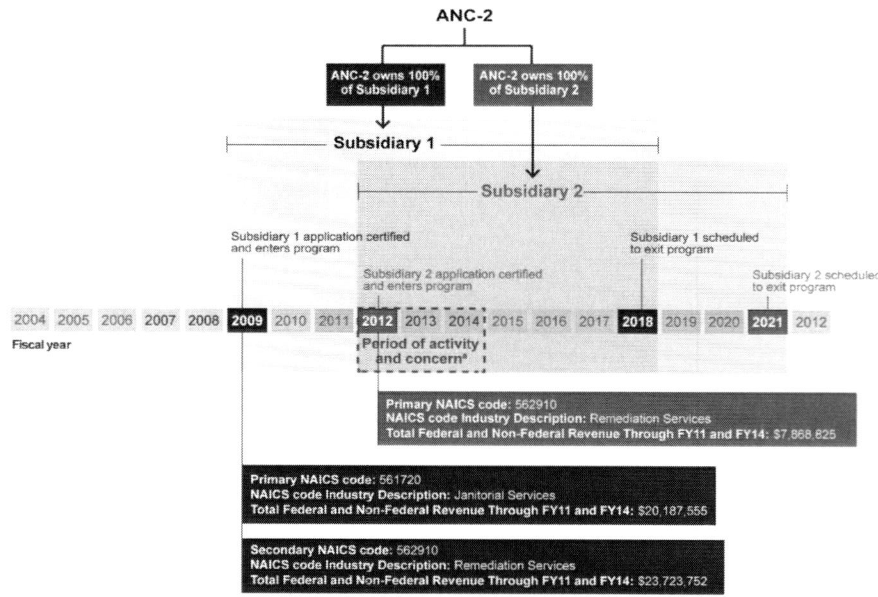

Source: GAO. | GAO-16-113

[a] Period of activity and concern: Through FY 2011 and FY 2014, ANC-2 fully owned Subsidiary-1 and Subsidiary 2. During this timeframe, Subsidiary-1 generated millions of dollars less in total revenue under its primary NAICS code 561720 than it generated under secondary NAICS code 562910, which was the same code used for Subsidiary-2's primary NAICS code.

Figure 6. Illustrative Example of Alaska Native Corporations (ANC)-owned Firms and their Use of NAICS Code in the 8(a) Program, Fiscal Years 2011-2014.

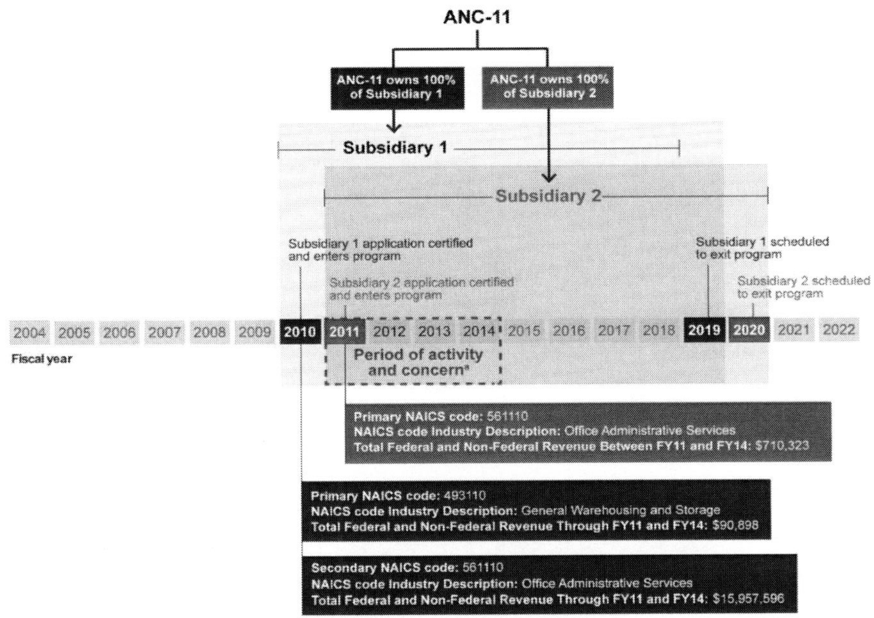

Source: GAO. | GAO-16-113.

[a] Period of activity and concern: Through FY 2011 and FY 2014, ANC-11 fully owned Subsidiary-1 and Subsidiary 2. During this timeframe, Subsidiary-1 generated millions of dollars less in total revenue under its primary NAICS code 493110 than it generated under secondary NAICS code 561110, which was the same code used for Subsidiary-2's primary NAICS code.

Figure 7. Illustrative Example of Alaska Native Corporations (ANC)-owned Firms and their Use of NAICS Code in the 8(a) Program, Fiscal Years 2011-2014.

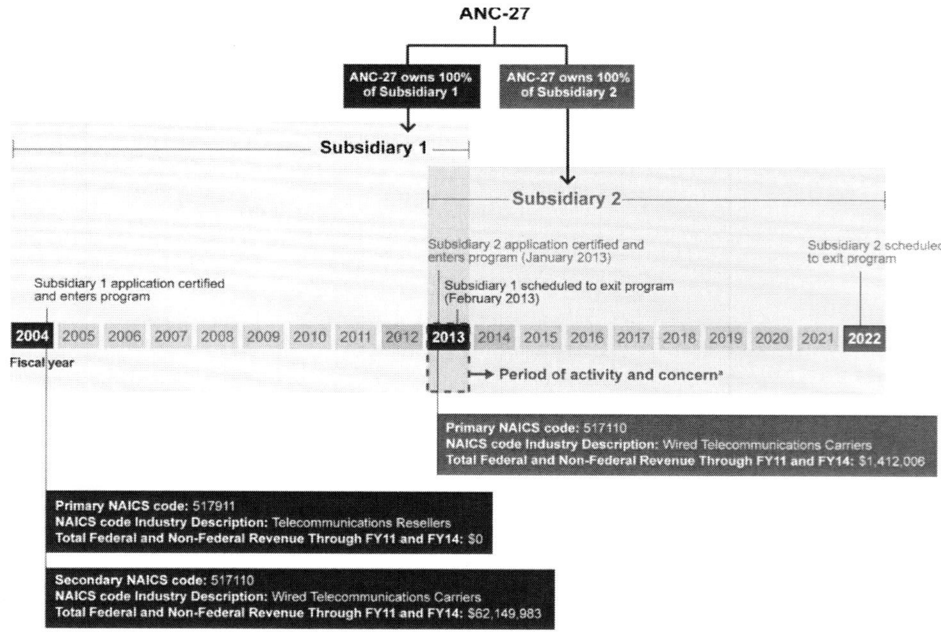

Source : GAO. | GAO-16-113

[a] Period of activity and concern: Through FY 2011 and FY 2013, ANC-27 fully owned Subsidiary-1 and Subsidiary 2. During this timeframe, Subsidiary-1 generated no revenue under its primary NAICS code 517911; however, it generated millions under secondary NAICS code 517110, which was the same code used for Subsidiary-2's primary NAICS code.

Figure 8. Illustrative Example of Alaska Native Corporations (ANC)-owned Firms and their Use of NAICS Code in the 8(a) Program, Fiscal Years 2011-2014.

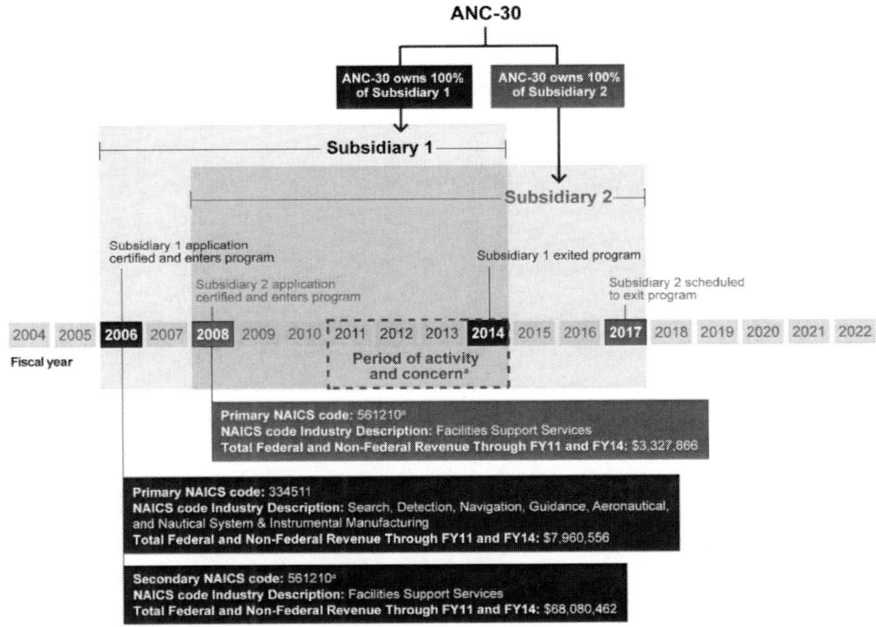

Source : GAO. | GAO-16-113.

[a] Period of activity and concern: Through FY 2011 and FY 2013, ANC-30 fully owned Subsidiary-1 and Subsidiary 2. During this timeframe, Subsidiary-1 generated millions less in total revenue under its primary NAICS code 334511 than it generated under secondary NAICS code 561210, which was the same code used for Subsidiary-2's primary NAICS code.

Figure 9. Illustrative Example of Alaska Native Corporations (ANC)-owned Firms and their Use of NAICS Code in the 8(a) Program, Fiscal Years 2011-2014.

APPENDIX IV: EXAMPLE OF AN ANC-OWNED 8(A) FIRM BENEFITS REPORTS SUBMISSION AND 8(A) REVENUES AND NON-PROGRAM REVENUES GENERATED BETWEEN 2011 AND 2014

In order to remain eligible for the 8(a) program, participating ANC-owned subsidiaries must submit information about their progress under the program, including benefits distributed to the native members or native community resulting from program participation as well as program and non-program revenues. Table 7 illustrates an example of an ANC-owned firm's annual submission of benefits, derived in part as a result of the firm's participation in the 8(a) program. Figure 6 describes the reported 8(a) revenues and non-8(a) revenues earned by the 26 8(a) participating ANC-owned firms between 2011 and 2014.

Table 8. Example of an 8(a) Program Related Distributions and Benefits Reported By One ANC-owned Firm in Fiscal Year 2012

Benefit data collection areas	Amount distributed (fiscal years 2010-2012)	Activities pursued
Employment	$3,000,000	The ANC continued efforts to provide support for a job and internship bank that benefits community members. The distribution of funds also contributed to compensation, fringe benefits, and taxes for employees.
Economic benefits	$1,100,000	The ANC distributed funds in the form of shareholder dividends, a settlement trust, and compensation for the Board of Directors.
Economic and community development	$455,000	Investments made to private and public infrastructure projects, housing, and construction jobs.
Health, social, and cultural support	$435,000	Distributions to this fund supported a range of programs including Youth Olympics, cultural camps, community garden, bereavement program, holiday dinners, and assuming the costs for life insurance premiums.

Benefit data collection areas	Amount distributed (fiscal years 2010-2012)	Activities pursued
Lands	$255,000	The ANC holds over 200,000 acres with an additional 70,000 acres to be conveyed. Distributions were made for the purposes of maintaining improved properties, security, and wildlife conservation.
Education and development	$105,000	Distributions made to provide for scholarships, grants, and elementary school trips.

Source: GAO analysis of ANC data. | GAO-16-113.

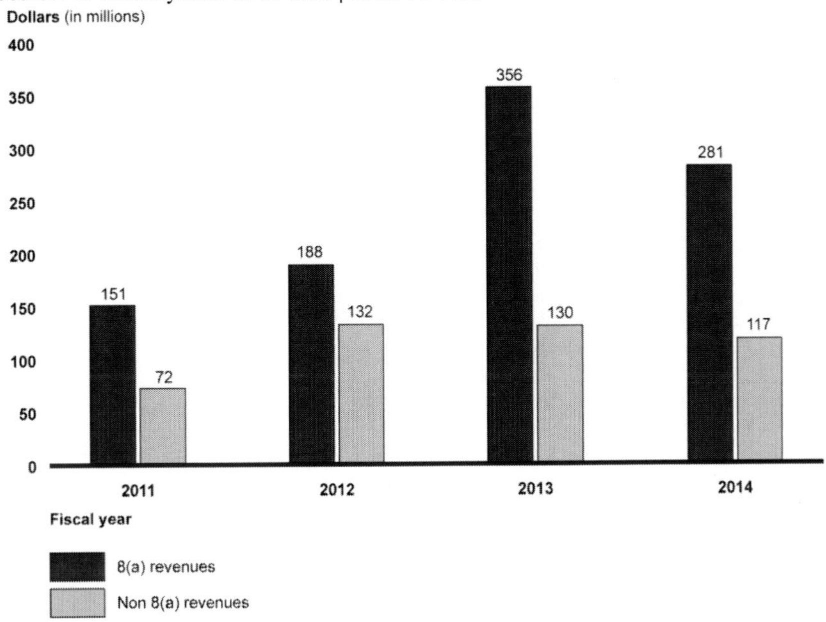

Source: GAO analysis of ANC Annual Updates. | GAO-16-113
Note-Totals are based on self-reported data submitted to SBA by the ANCs.
[a] Not all 26 8(a) ANC-owned firms provided annual reviews during 2011-2014.

Figure 10. Self-Reported 8(a) and Non-8(a) Revenues for the Reviewed 26 8(a) ANC-owned firms, 2011-2014a.

End Notes

[1] Under SBA's regulations, ANCs are defined as any Regional Corporation, Village Corporation, Urban Corporation, or Group Corporation organized under the laws of the State of Alaska

in accordance with the Alaska Native Claims Settlement Act, as amended. 13 C.F.R. § 124.3. In this report, the term "ANC" refers to the one of these parent corporations, usually located in Alaska. The term "ANC-owned firm" denotes a business owned by an ANC. This term has the same meaning as "ANC-owned concern," which is the term used in SBA's small-business regulations. We also use the term "sister subsidiary," "ANC-owned subsidiary," and "ANC-owned firms" to refer to wholly and partially owned subsidiaries of ANCs.

[2] An obligation is a binding agreement that will result in financial outlays, immediately or in the future. Budgetary resources must be available before obligations can be incurred legally. In this report, the term "obligation" refers to the annual expenditure for particular contracts, and not the total award amount.

[3] Although many of these advantages also apply to Indian tribes, Native Hawaiian Organizations, and Community Development Corporations, in this report we focus exclusively on the rules as applied to ANC-owned firms participating in the 8(a) program. Congress initially passed legislation in 1986 that allowed ANC owned firms to participate in SBA's 8(a) program, and subsequent laws established and clarified their advantages in the program. Unlike most other 8(a) small businesses, ANC-owned firms receive an exclusion from affiliation with their larger parent corporation and therefore can be subsidiaries in large corporations that may have worldwide operation, annually generate revenues in the hundreds of millions of dollars, and provide a range of goods and services to federal procuring agencies.

[4] Participating 8(a) firms must qualify as "small" under an industry size standard as measured by the average number of employees over the past 12 months or average revenues generated from the previous 3 years, in addition to being majority-owned by a disadvantaged individual or a qualified entity, such as an ANC. According to the Small Business Act, a business is considered small when it is independently owned and operated; is not dominant in its field of operations; and meets any definitions or standards established by the Administrator of SBA. Overall, SBA considers more than 97 percent of all businesses to be "small," and these firms represent about 30 percent of industry receipts.

[5] 76 Fed. Reg. 8222 (Feb. 11, 2011).

[6] GAO, *Federal Contracting: Monitoring and Oversight of Tribal 8(a) Firms Need Attention,* GAO-12-84, (Washington, D.C.: Jan. 31, 2012).

[7] SBA did not comment on the recommendations made in that report when issued. In all, we made seven recommendations in GAO-12-84, three of the seven recommendations, including the recommendation to provide a full acquisition history in offer letters and direct business opportunity specialist to focus on this issue when conducting their reviews, have been fully implemented as of October 2015. We discuss this particular recommendation in more detail in objective 1. The other four recommendations are related to issues noted with monitoring subcontractors under the program, joint venture projects, and reporting on unfair competitive advantages to Congress are outside the scope of this report.

[8] In line with federal standards on internal controls, control environment factors include the program's organizational structure and delegation of authority and responsibility, human capital policies and practices that affect the program, and management's commitment to competence as well as its philosophy and operating style, among other things.

[9] FPDS-NG is the central repository for U.S. government procurement data. Individuals and entities awarded contracts with an estimated value of $3,000 or more must submit detailed contract information to FPDS-NG. The database includes the product or service, agency and vendor information, contract start and expiration dates, and location of performance, among other elements. We did not generate a sample or selection for objective 4. This research objective focuses on management challenges we identified while conducting our analyses for the other three research objectives.

[10] See our methodological discussion of objective 2 in the Objective, Scope, and Methodology section (appendix I) of this report.

[11] Under certain circumstances, procuring departments and agencies may award an 8(a) contract at or below $150,000 without providing previous notification to SBA. Once an award has been made, however, the department or agency is required to notify SBA of the contract.13 C.F.R. §§ 124.501(a) and 124.503(a)(4)(ii).

[12] Our analysis of the selected variables from FPDS-NG that may indicate that the contract is a sole-source follow-on to an ANC sister subsidiary yielded results for the remaining 102 contracts. However, our more detailed review revealed that our methodology did not reliability identify cases that were truly follow-on, sole-source contracts to sister subsidiaries. For this reason, and other reasons described later in the report, we did not pursue further analysis of all of the cases.

[13] The North American Industry Classification System (NAICS) is the standard used by federal statistical agencies in classifying business establishments for the purpose of collecting, analyzing, and publishing statistical data related to the U.S. business economy. NAICS codes were developed under the auspices of the Office of Management and Budget, and adopted in 1997 to replace the Standard Industrial Classification (SIC) system. Each solicitation for a federal procurement, above the micro-purchase level, is assigned an NAICS code that best describes the goods or services being acquired and the principal purpose of the procurement. Each NAICS code has a corresponding size standard and SBA establishes small business size standards on an industry-by-industry basis. Size standards are set forth in 13 C.F.R. Part 121 and generally are expressed in dollars or average number of full-time employees. Some NAICS codes include one or more subcategories of work with different corresponding size standards. SBA's Office of Size Standards has identified that these subcategories are different enough to warrant separate recognition and that the industries are different enough to warrant distinct size standards. As such, two ANC-owned sister subsidiaries may share the same primary high- level NAICS code as long as they do not share the same subcategory with corresponding size standard.

[14] SAM is the official U.S. government system that maintains records on all federal prime contractors and is overseen by GSA. We used this system to identify primary NAICS codes. SBA's DSBS is a searchable database that includes uploaded registration data that small businesses—including those participants of the 8(a) program—initially entered into SAM. DSBS is used by contracting officials to identify potential small business contractors for upcoming contracting opportunities.

[15] In all, there were 53 parent ANCs with at least one subsidiary firm participating in the 8(a) program.

[16] GAO, *Agency Performance Plans: Examples of Practices That Can Improve Usefulness to Decision-makers*, GAO/GGD/AIMD-99-69 (Washington, D.C.: Feb. 26, 1999).

[17] This was out of the 665 firms that participated in the 8(a) program during that period.

[18] While all four firms excluded from our analysis were categorized in FPDS-NG as ANC- owned firms, three of the four firms were owned by individuals who were Alaska Natives. Under the rules, these firms are not considered ANC-owned firms. However, they are considered to be firms owned by disadvantaged individuals. The fourth firm was also owned by a disadvantaged individual, but was not an Alaska Native.

[19] GAO, *Standards for Internal Control in the Federal Government*, GAO/AIMD-00-21.3.1, (Washington, D.C.: November 1999).

[20] GAO, *Human Capital: Key Principles for Effective Strategic Workforce Planning*, GAO-04-39 (Washington, D.C.: Dec. 11, 2003).

[21] A set-aside is an acquisition reserved exclusively for participation by small business concerns. These may be awarded to SBA for performance by eligible 8(a) firms on either a competitive or sole-source basis. A sole-source award is a contract awarded, or proposed for award, without competition.

[22] Wholly-owned ANC subsidiary firms comprised the majority (23 of 26) of firms we selected for one segment of our review. The remaining three were partnerships where an ANC owned the majority of the firm with non-ANC owners.

[23] On the annual update, firms are expected to report whether there have been any changes in partnership agreements, articles of incorporation, by-laws, or stock issues since the firm received certification and that have not been previously reported to SBA.

[24] 13 C.F.R. §124.2. If SBA certifies the firm, the firm remains certified for no more than 9 years from the date of SBA's approval letter. During this 9-year term, the 8(a) participant must maintain its program eligibility and must inform SBA of any changes that would adversely affect its program eligibility. A business can be approved to participate in the 8(a) program only one time.

[25] While all 8(a) firms report annually to SBA, they are expected to time the updates of their progress on the anniversary of their entry date into the program. Throughout this report, we will present findings and data in terms of program year or fiscal year, as stated. When not explicitly stated, we are referring to a calendar year.

[26] Through partnership agreements between SBA and procuring agencies, SBA may delegate some responsibility for contract execution and administration to the contracting officers at the procuring agencies.

[27] Each federal department and agency is expected to set annual goals for procurement contracts awarded to small businesses, small disadvantaged businesses, women-owned small businesses, HUBZone small businesses and service-disabled veteran-owned small businesses. SBA is responsible for ensuring that the government-wide goal for participation of small business concerns is established annually at the statutory levels and the reporting agencies' achievements are relative to the goals.

[28] 76 Fed. Reg. 8222 (Feb. 11, 2011). According to SBA, the regulatory changes were the first comprehensive revision to the 8(a) program in more than 10 years. The changes ranged from technical changes to substantive clarifications of program rules that reflected the SBA's experiences in implementing the regulations.

[29] In this report, we focus on the regulatory updates related to changes in follow-on, sole- source contracts, sharing NAICS codes and all changes related to ownership, compensation, excessive withdrawals and benefits reporting.

[30] The change made to this particular regulation was a technical update to the language previously in effect since 1998.

[31] GAO-12-84.

[32] An offer letter is an official notification to SBA by a procuring agency that intends to award a contract under the 8(a) Business Development program. 13 C.F.R. § 124.502(c). Regulations that outline what information must be included were in place prior to the revisions in SBA's 2011 final rule.

[33] As we previously mentioned in this report, our final analysis evaluated 30 large value contracts—or contracts valued over the $150,000 SAP threshold because agencies may not enter into such contracts without first providing information to SBA. While our analysis ultimately revealed that the contract activities for these 30 cases were unrelated and thus, not follow-on, sole source contracts; we did identify challenges to SBA's ability to identify sole source contracts and enforce its prohibition against them. See table 1 for our previous discussion of our selection methodology.

[34] GAO-12-84. Based on our discussion with officials, SBA has had difficulty in launching the systems we recommended that would enable SBA to track relationships between 8(a) contracts, and thus more readily identify potential sole-source, follow-on contracts improperly awarded to ANC sister subsidiaries. We address this issue in greater detail later in this report.

[35] As an additional step, and in order to obtain the missing documentation, we contacted some of the federal procuring departments and agencies directly related to these contracts. In the 30 cases we reviewed, we found that the contract activities were unrelated. However, SBA did not maintain sufficient documentation in order to make this same determination for some of the contracts we selected.

[36] GAO/AIMD-00-21.3.1.

[37] To facilitate our review of the missing documents, we asked the procuring agency to provide us with copies of available materials from their files.

[38] See GAO, *Contract Management: Increased Use of Alaska Native Corporations' Special 8(a) Provisions Calls for Tailored Oversight*, GAO-06-399 (Washington, D.C.: Apr. 27, 2006).

[39] GAO-12-84.

[40] Some NAICS codes include one or more subcategories of work with different corresponding size standards. Two sister subsidiaries may share the same primary high- level NAICS code as long as they do not share the same subcategory with corresponding size standard. For purposes of this report, when we refer to SBA's prohibition against sister subsidiaries sharing primary NAICS codes, we mean it to include this subcategory distinction when relevant for the particular code.

[41] As a condition for continued participation in the program, 8(a) firms are to submit information such as total amounts of all 8(a) and non-8(a) revenues, compensation, and benefits distributed to the community in their annual reviews.

[42] GAO-06-399. We later closed this recommendation as not implemented.

[43] GAO-12-84. However, as we found then and now, SBA's current systems that track 8(a) participant data do not collect or track revenue that sister subsidiaries generate under all primary and secondary NAICS codes.

[44] In February 2014, SBA's Office of Inspector General (OIG) found that SBA failed to follow federal acquisition rules and guidance during the acquisition process of this database. According to the OIG, this resulted in SBA acquiring a system that would have insufficient capabilities not aligned with what it had originally designed. SBA OIG, *The SBA Did Not Follow Federal Regulations and Guidance in the Acquisition of the One Track System,* rpt. no. 14-10 (February 2014).

[45] The proposed rule would give some discretion to SBA and afford subsidiaries an opportunity to provide information explaining why such a change would be inappropriate. However, four ANCs told us that they do not support the proposed rule as written as they are concerned that it could give SBA authority to automatically change an ANC-owned subsidiary's primary NAICS code without any formal review or corrective action process.

[46] According to SBA officials, these continuing eligibility reviews will involve centralized staff conducting oversight that will involve reviewing and certifying that the subsidiaries continue to be eligible to participate in the 8(a) program.

[47] GAO did not review SBA's draft plan, which SBA officials indicated had not yet been finalized.

[48] GAO/GGD/AIMD-99-69.

[49] GAO/AIMD-00-21.3.1.

[50] This strategy includes creating a new and centralized SBA office that would be responsible for conducting deeper reviews to support the district offices' monitoring efforts.

[51] These 26 firms were randomly selected from all 8(a) ANC-owned firms participating in the program from calendar years 2011 through 2014.

[52] SBA expects that all responses whether submitted by individual participating firms or a parent corporation will correlate to the financial statements submitted each year to SBA. In total there are seven categories.

[53] SBA-OIG, rpt. No. 9-15.

[54] A primary reason for the variation is that SBA does not have a standard form through which to collect this information. In 2011, SBA developed a seven page form, but SBA and the Office of Management and Budget (OMB) received comments that the form was too burdensome and it was not adopted. After consultations with OMB, ANCs, and other groups, SBA proposed a new one page form in June 2015. As this report was being issued, OMB approved the form on March 3, 2016. Officials indicated that the form is scheduled to be published in June 2016.

[55] A program year marks the specific date of the firm's entry into SBA's 8(a) Business Development Program.

[56] Federal procurement obligations can comprise most if not all of an ANC-owned firm's profits while participating in the 8(a) program.

[57] The Alaska District Office services over half of all ANC-owned firms participating in the 8(a) program.

[58] 13 C.F.R. § 124.112(b)(5).

[59] That is, the number of participant firms that provided data for all available years in which a participant firm could provide data. Five of the 26 firms did not participate in all 4 years of our analysis, either entering the program at some point after 2011 or exiting the program at some point before or during 2014.

[60] 13 C.F.R § 124.112(d)(1).

[61] SBA may initiate termination proceeding against 8(a) participants for excessive withdrawals that are detrimental to the achievement of the targets, objectives, and goals contained in the participating firm's business plan, including transfers of funds or other business assets from the concern for the personal benefit of any of its owners or managers, or any person or entity affiliated with the owners or managers. 13 C.F.R. § 124.303(a)(13).

[62] 13 C.F.R § 124.112(d)(3).

[63] SBA did not meet this deadline. In an update to GAO, a SBA official indicated that the guidance would be issued instead by mid-March 2016.

[64] GAO, *Assessing the Reliability of Computer-Processed Data,* GAO-09-680G (Washington, D.C.: July 2009).

[65] GAO-09-680G.

[66] GAO/AIMD-00-21.3.1.

[67] We reviewed these files for our analysis of ownership, compensation, profits and distributed benefits data. The findings in this section are limited to the Alaska District Office.

[68] One of the objectives of the review is to monitor a firm's growth and progress towards attaining the ability to compete in the open market without SBA's assistance.

[69] An annual review set consists of the four annual review updates that would be provided by each participating 8(a) ANC owned firm to SBA for the period 2011 through 2014.

[70] According to program guidance and upon completion of the annual review analysis, a business opportunity specialist is to forward the document to the assistant district director and then on to the district director for final approval of a firm's continued eligibility.

[71] GAO-06-399. In 2006, we noted that the shortages in staffing and limited contracting acumen affected SBA's ability to provide adequate oversight, and we recommended that SBA evaluate staffing levels and take steps to allocate the appropriate levels of staff to this office. While SBA addressed this recommendation, our site visit in 2014 revealed that the problem with the appropriate level of staffing at the Alaska District Office remains a concern.

[72] At the time of our initial site visit to Anchorage, Alaska in October 2014, the district office also had a part-time business opportunity specialist assigned to monitor firms. However, we were told at that time that this individual was still in training to assume these responsibilities. When we returned to Anchorage, Alaska, in April of the following year, the 8(a) program had hired two additional staff, bringing the number of business opportunity specialists to 2.5 full time equivalent employees (the number of employees on full-time schedules plus the number of employees on part-time schedules converted to a full-time basis).

[73] SBA, OIG, *Non-Native Managers Secured Millions of Dollars from 8(a) Firms Owned by Alaska Native Corporations through Unapproved Agreements That Jeopardized the Firms' Program Eligibility*, rpt. no. 8-14 (August 2008) and GAO-06-399.

[74] SBA conducted a VERA/VSIP between 2012 and 2014. A VERA allows agencies that are undergoing substantial restructuring, reshaping, downsizing, transferring of function, or reorganization to temporarily lower the age and service requirements in order to increase the number of employees who are eligible for retirement. The authority encourages more voluntary separations and helps the agency complete the needed organizational change with minimal disruption to the work force. By offering these short term opportunities, an agency

can make it possible for employees to receive an immediate annuity years before they would otherwise be eligible. Chief Human Capital Officers Act of 2002 (Pub. L. No. 107-296, Title XIII, § 1313, 116 Stat. 2135, 2291 (2002)).

[75] According to officials, this office oversees the operations of SBA's 68 district offices nationwide including staffing and monitoring for performance. The Alaska District Office has five additional staff responsible for a variety of tasks and includes the district director and deputy, marketing and administrative staff.

[76] We first placed the management of federal human capital on our High Risk List in 2001, see GAO, *High-Risk Series: An Update,* GAO-01-263 (Washington, D.C.: January 2001). In 2013, we also said that the Office of Personnel Management should continue its efforts to include addressing government-wide mission critical skills gaps in occupations such as contracting and procurement. See GAO, *High-Risk Series: An Update,* GAO-13-283 (Washington, D.C.: February 2013).

[77] Succession plans address the entity's need to replace competent personnel over the long term, whereas contingency plans address the entity's need to respond to sudden personnel changes that could compromise the internal control system. GAO-04-39. Additionally, federal internal control guidance suggests that agencies develop succession and contingency plans for key roles to help the entity continue achieving its objectives despite organizational transformations. GAO/AIMD-00-21.3.1.

[78] SBA, OIG, rpt. no. 8-14.

[79] SBA, OIG, rpt. no. 9-15.

[80] We asked SBA officials for a copy of their findings and we were told that none of the findings had been formally documented.

[81] Pub. L. No 100-656, Title II, § 201, 102 Stat. 3853, 3856 - 3858.

[82] According to SBA, and pursuant to the authority in 15 U.S.C. § 636(j)(11)(F)(iv) and (v), the continuing eligibility review unit will have responsibility to review and evaluate financial statements and other submissions from firms participating in the 8(a) program to ascertain continued eligibility to receive subcontracts and to make a request for the initiation of termination or graduation proceedings, as appropriate.

[83] SBA officials reported that the new unit will be called the Office of Certification and Eligibility.

[84] GAO/AIMD-00-21.3.1.

[85] In line with federal standards on internal controls, the control environment factors include the program's organizational structure and delegation of authority and responsibility, human capital policies and practices that affect the program, management's commitment to competence as well as its philosophy and operating style, among other things. Information management controls determines through assessments and monitoring that relevant, reliable, and timely information is available for management decision making and external reporting purposes.

[86] FPDS-NG is the central repository for U.S. government procurement data. Individuals and entities awarded contracts with an estimated value of $3,000 or more must submit detailed contract information to FPDS-NG. The database includes the product or service, agency and vendor information, contract start and expiration dates, and location of performance, among other elements. We did not generate a sample or selection for Objective 4. This research objective focuses on management challenges we identified while conducting our analyses for the other three research objectives.

[87] As we noted elsewhere in this report, SBA's DSBS is a searchable database that includes uploaded registration data that small businesses initially enter into SAM, including NAICS code information and entrance and exit dates for the 8(a) program. DSBS data are used by federal contracting officials to identify potential small business contractors for upcoming contracting opportunities. GSA's SAM is the official federal system that ANC subsidiaries are generally required to register before they conduct 8(a) business with federal agencies or departments. ANC subsidiaries are also required to use SAM to self-report and attest to

certain information, including the primary and secondary NAICS codes used. SAM assists ANC subsidiaries with obtaining 8(a) contract opportunities because federal procuring agencies and departments use SAM data when awarding contracts or for past performance reporting and suspension and debarment information.

[88] We reviewed these 30 contract files to corroborate the indication from FPDS-NG that these contracts had the potential to be follow-on, sole-source contracts. Our results indicate that the variables we selected from FPDS-NG were not adequate indicators, and we found that such determinations can only be made by detailed review of each case file.

[89] GSA's FPDS-NG is a federal automated system used to collect and report on federal procurement spending; it is the single authoritative repository for federal procurement award data. FPDS-NG data is submitted via a contract writing system or directly into FPDS-NG using direct web input; reports can be run by individuals.

[90] In all there were a total 53 ANCs owning at least one firm that participated in the program from fiscal year 2011 through 2014.

[91] SBA's regulation limits ANCs from owning multiple subsidiaries operating under the same primary line of business (i.e. under the same primary NAICS code) at the time of application into the 8(a) program or within the previous two years. SBA updated its regulations effective March 2011 by, among other things, replacing the word "SIC" with "NAICS" to reflect the industry's transition from using SIC codes to NAICS codes.

[92] GAO/AIMD-00-21.3.1.

[93] GAO-04-39.

INDEX

#

8(a) business development program, vii, 1
8(a) contracting, vii, 1, 2, 6, 7, 31, 51, 56, 59, 62
8(a) Program Requirements, v
8(a) regulation, vii, 1, 3, 5, 14, 33, 51, 54, 56, 87

A

access, 33, 38, 39, 47, 48, 55, 66, 67, 86, 92, 93, 94, 110, 112, 116
accountability, 29, 67, 106, 111, 115
acquisitions, 4, 6, 9, 63
administrative support, 46, 75
agencies, vii, 1, 2, 3, 5, 6, 8, 13, 18, 21, 29, 31, 32, 36, 37, 38, 42, 48, 51, 52, 53, 54, 55, 56, 57, 59, 61, 62, 66, 68, 69, 70, 71, 77, 78, 79, 80, 81, 82, 83, 84, 85, 86, 102, 104, 105, 109, 110, 111, 113, 120, 134, 135, 136, 138, 139
Air Force, 30, 32, 58
Alaska, i, iii, v, vii, 1, 2, 3, 4, 5, 32, 38, 43, 45, 56, 60, 63, 65, 66, 67, 68, 69, 73, 75, 80, 82, 83, 84, 94, 95, 96, 98, 100, 102, 103, 104, 105, 106, 107, 111, 115, 123, 124, 125, 126, 127, 128, 129, 130, 131, 133, 135, 137, 138, 139
Alaska Native Corporation (ANC), v, vii, 1, 2, 3, 4, 5, 6, 7, 8, 9, 10, 11, 15, 16, 29, 36, 37, 38, 41, 42, 43, 47, 48, 49, 50, 51, 56, 57, 59, 60, 62, 63, 65, 66, 67, 68, 69, 70, 71, 72, 73, 75, 76, 77, 78, 79, 80, 81, 82, 84, 85, 86, 87, 88, 89, 91, 92, 93, 94, 95, 96, 97, 98, 99, 100, 101, 102, 103, 104, 105, 106, 107, 108, 109, 110, 111, 112, 113, 115, 117, 118, 119, 120, 121, 122, 123, 124, 125, 126, 127, 128, 129, 130, 131, 132, 133, 134, 135, 136, 137, 138, 139
annual review, 7, 31, 45, 49, 60, 77, 86, 87, 98, 99, 100, 101, 102, 103, 104, 107, 112, 115, 121, 123, 125, 133, 137, 138
appropriations, 19, 61
Appropriations Act, 61
assessment, 28, 40, 103, 116
audit, 7, 28, 55, 60, 62, 72, 74, 91, 95, 109, 113, 121, 122, 124
authority, 61, 77, 78, 88, 91, 120, 134, 137, 138, 139
average revenue, 8, 48, 134

B

base, 19, 20, 27, 30, 32, 34, 35, 48, 57

basic ordering agreement (BOA), 3, 20, 53, 61
benefits, 2, 4, 7, 14, 21, 29, 30, 60, 68, 69, 70, 78, 79, 94, 95, 102, 112, 117, 118, 122, 123, 132, 136, 137, 138
board members, 46
bonuses, 97, 99
Bureau of Customs and Border Protection, 59
Business Development Management Information System (BDMIS), 67, 88, 93, 94
businesses, 3, 4, 5, 8, 10, 13, 30, 35, 36, 39, 45, 47, 48, 51, 52, 54, 55, 56, 60, 61, 62, 68, 69, 72, 74, 81, 82, 87, 89, 95, 110, 134, 135, 136, 139

C

certification, 61, 75, 117, 136
challenges, 26, 28, 54, 65, 70, 73, 84, 86, 92, 101, 105, 107, 115, 117, 123, 134, 136, 139
clarity, 31, 51, 55
classification, 10, 88
Code of Federal Regulations, 59, 80
commercial, 61, 91
community, 4, 5, 14, 45, 55, 69, 79, 95, 99, 102, 112, 132, 137
community service, 4
compensation, 13, 69, 70, 73, 78, 94, 96, 97, 98, 99, 100, 101, 102, 112, 117, 118, 122, 123, 132, 136, 137, 138
competition, 2, 18, 20, 22, 24, 25, 29, 30, 61, 69, 135
competitive advantage, 9, 41, 43, 44, 51, 53, 134
competitors, 47, 48
compliance, vii, 1, 3, 5, 13, 30, 31, 32, 33, 34, 36, 38, 52, 55, 56, 59, 62, 63, 67, 69, 70, 73, 77, 93, 95, 100, 108, 110, 111, 112, 123
complications, 105
conflict, 5, 23, 45, 67
Congress, 4, 8, 45, 51, 53, 68, 134
conservation, 133
construction, 12, 13, 20, 27, 29, 30, 32, 42, 43, 48, 49, 61, 98, 132
contingency, 139
coordination, 116
cost, 24, 25, 26, 28, 29, 48
cost saving, 29
counseling, 74
customer service, 115
Customs and Border Protection, 59

D

data collection, 2, 52, 55, 67, 86, 100, 132, 133
Data Universal Numbering System (DUNS), 3, 6, 57, 63
database, 2, 3, 51, 52, 56, 65, 70, 71, 83, 88, 93, 94, 112, 120, 134, 135, 137, 139
Defense Contract Audit Agency (DCAA), 3, 28, 40, 62
deficiencies, 85, 101, 106, 110
Department of Agriculture, 34, 58
Department of Defense (DOD), 3, 9, 19, 20, 28, 29, 34, 57, 58, 61, 62
Department of Energy, 23, 30, 58, 62
Department of Homeland Security, 19, 59
Department of Justice, 34, 59
Department of Labor, 59
development assistance, 8
directives, 92, 94
directors, 10, 46, 96, 97, 98
distribution, 13, 70, 73, 84, 117, 118, 122, 132
Division of Program Certification and Eligibility (DPCE), 67, 87
documentary evidence, 121, 123
downsizing, 138
draft, 53, 85, 92, 100, 102, 104, 105, 109, 112, 137
Drug Enforcement Administration, 59

Dynamic Small Business Search (DSBS), 57, 67, 72, 119, 121, 122, 135, 139

E

economic activity, 61
economic development, 45, 60, 105, 115
economic disadvantage, 9, 10
employees, 8, 9, 12, 13, 20, 23, 30, 31, 33, 34, 39, 48, 49, 63, 78, 97, 132, 134, 135, 138
employment, 20, 60, 95
enforcement, 84, 94, 102, 103, 104, 111, 113
engineering, 19, 20, 32
enrollment, 86, 87
environment, 2, 18, 24, 27, 29, 48, 104, 108, 134, 139
environment factors, 134, 139
equipment, 23, 26
evidence, 7, 31, 33, 38, 60, 62, 74, 104, 121, 123, 124
exclusion, 61, 134
execution, 77, 83, 120, 136
expertise, 74, 104, 123

F

family members, 99
Federal Acquisition Regulation (FAR), 3, 5, 6, 7, 20, 23, 25, 32, 33, 52, 55, 56, 59, 60, 61, 62, 67, 113
Federal Bureau of Investigation, 59
Federal Emergency Management Agency, 30, 59
federal government, 4, 29, 48, 61, 68
Federal Government, 135
financial, 11, 33, 40, 50, 62, 74, 93, 100, 102, 108, 134, 137, 139
financial development, 75
fiscal year, 2, 4, 6, 8, 14, 15, 16, 18, 19, 56, 57, 61, 65, 68, 70, 71, 72, 73, 79, 80, 85, 89, 104, 108, 109, 113, 119, 121, 122, 126, 132, 133, 136, 140
fluctuations, 91
Food and Drug Administration, 35, 59
fraud, 54, 103
fringe benefits, 132
funding, 28, 95
funds, 95, 99, 132, 138

G

GAO, 1, 2, 3, 8, 11, 12, 15, 16, 17, 43, 44, 50, 60, 61, 62, 63, 65, 66, 67, 72, 75, 76, 80, 81, 84, 90, 97, 101, 104, 107, 115, 118, 125, 127, 128, 129, 130, 131, 133, 134, 135, 136, 137, 138, 139, 140
General Services Administration(GSA), 3, 26, 67, 71, 135, 139, 140
goods and services, 4, 134
government policy, 61
government procurement, 134, 139
grants, 133
gross domestic product, 57
growth, 2, 14, 45, 48, 49, 51, 87, 88, 138
guidance, 2, 29, 31, 32, 33, 52, 55, 59, 67, 72, 73, 82, 83, 84, 85, 86, 96, 99, 100, 101, 103, 106, 109, 110, 111, 112, 113, 114, 121, 123, 137, 138, 139

H

Hawaii, 7, 60
Health and Human Services, 6, 53
hiring, 31, 34, 105, 106
history, 5, 13, 22, 38, 47, 51, 53, 54, 66, 70, 79, 81, 82, 83, 85, 113, 114, 134
holding company, 7
House of Representatives, 68
human, 74, 105, 107, 115, 123, 134, 139
human capital, 74, 105, 107, 115, 123, 134, 139

I

identification, 63
imbalances, 116
improvements, 55, 107, 113
income, 11, 42, 92, 116
Indian tribes, vii, 1, 4, 5, 6, 7, 8, 14, 54, 56, 57, 60, 134
individuals, 4, 5, 8, 10, 11, 13, 63, 69, 71, 95, 97, 119, 124, 135, 140
industry(ies), 8, 9, 10, 11, 41, 42, 43, 46, 47, 50, 51, 52, 53, 56, 61, 63, 70, 88, 91, 92, 98, 110, 116, 134, 135, 140
inflation, 15, 17, 57
information sharing, 93
information technology, 37
infrastructure, 132
initiation, 99, 139
integrity, 102, 111
internal controls, 73, 102, 110, 111, 112, 115, 117, 119, 123, 134, 139
issues, 3, 21, 35, 41, 51, 54, 70, 73, 74, 86, 107, 108, 115, 118, 122, 124, 134, 136

J

joint ventures, 3, 35, 39, 40, 53, 57, 63
justification, 5, 19, 23, 24, 29, 60

L

laws, 11, 63, 93, 133, 134, 136
laws and regulations, 11, 93
leadership, 108, 109
legislation, 4, 9, 134
lifetime, 9, 41

M

magnitude, 109
majority, 2, 3, 4, 6, 8, 10, 14, 38, 39, 40, 41, 42, 53, 56, 57, 61, 63, 69, 70, 75, 88, 124, 134, 135
management, 10, 11, 22, 30, 45, 46, 48, 55, 63, 70, 73, 75, 92, 94, 102, 109, 115, 117, 124, 134, 139
manufacturing, 4, 6, 9, 63, 69
marketing, 18, 21, 37, 48, 77, 139
marketing strategy, 18
marketplace, 29, 49
materials, 21, 33, 37, 120, 125, 137
Medicaid, 34, 59
medical, 20, 22, 30
Medicare, 34, 58
mentor, 13, 39, 40, 57, 61, 63
mentoring, 74, 102, 104, 115, 117
methodology, 2, 7, 60, 74, 135, 136
Mexico, 7, 58, 60
mission, 73, 105, 139
modifications, 83, 121

N

National Defense Authorization Act, 5, 23, 60
Native Hawaiian Organization (NHO), vii, 1, 4, 9, 10, 11, 15, 16, 50, 56, 57, 60, 134
native population, 5
negotiating, 26, 28
negotiation, 27, 29, 32, 34, 59, 62
NHOs, 4, 5, 6, 7, 8, 14, 56, 57, 62
North America, 3, 12, 68, 72, 121, 135
North American Industry Classification System (NAICS), 3, 12, 13, 20, 21, 41, 42, 61, 63, 68, 72, 78, 87, 88, 89, 90, 91, 92, 93, 94, 101, 109, 110, 112, 116, 118, 121, 123, 126, 127, 128, 129, 130, 131, 135, 136, 137, 139, 140

O

Office of Federal Procurement Policy (OFPP), 2, 4, 7, 52, 53, 55
Office of Inspector General (OIG), 68, 95, 104, 106, 119, 137, 138, 139
Office of Management and Budget (OMB), 4, 19, 29, 61, 62, 135, 137
officials, 1, 2, 3, 5, 6, 7, 18, 19, 20, 21, 22, 23, 24, 25, 27, 28, 29, 30, 31, 32, 33, 34, 35, 36, 37, 38, 39, 40, 42, 44, 45, 48, 50, 51, 52, 53, 55, 56, 57, 59, 60, 61, 62, 63, 66, 70, 73, 78, 80, 81, 82, 84, 85, 86, 87, 88, 91, 92, 93, 94, 95, 97, 98, 100, 101, 102, 104, 105, 106, 107, 108, 110, 111, 113, 114, 116, 119, 120, 122, 123, 135, 136, 137, 139
operations, 7, 10, 11, 63, 102, 110, 134, 139
opportunities, 29, 50, 61, 76, 85, 89, 91, 106, 135, 138, 139
oversight, vii, 1, 5, 6, 12, 51, 52, 56, 59, 65, 67, 70, 73, 77, 82, 84, 85, 86, 88, 93, 94, 100, 101, 102, 103, 104, 105, 106, 107, 110, 111, 112, 113, 115, 117, 119, 123, 137, 138
ownership, 13, 32, 73, 75, 77, 78, 122, 123, 124, 136, 138

P

participants, 8, 38, 41, 49, 63, 66, 68, 69, 85, 97, 101, 124, 135, 138
per capita income, 11
personal benefit, 138
personnel costs, 12, 13, 30, 33, 34
policy, 29, 44, 51, 53, 61, 108, 110
population, 6, 11, 54, 57, 60, 71, 72, 73, 119, 121, 123
preparation, 35, 43
price competition, 25
price determinations, vii, 1, 5, 56
primary data, 119
principles, 116
private sector, 19, 98
procurement, 5, 13, 19, 21, 22, 27, 32, 37, 38, 39, 53, 56, 60, 61, 66, 70, 74, 77, 82, 83, 84, 85, 113, 114, 134, 135, 136, 138, 139, 140
profit, 4, 9, 12, 13, 25, 75

Q

quality control, 119

R

recommendations, 2, 5, 30, 31, 51, 54, 55, 66, 107, 110, 112, 116, 134
redistribution, 107
regulations, 2, 3, 5, 6, 11, 12, 13, 14, 20, 22, 30, 32, 33, 35, 36, 37, 38, 39, 40, 41, 45, 51, 52, 53, 54, 59, 60, 62, 63, 65, 66, 69, 70, 71, 73, 77, 78, 79, 81, 83, 84, 85, 86, 87, 89, 92, 93, 96, 99, 100, 103, 109, 110, 112, 116, 117, 118, 119, 120, 123, 133, 136, 140
regulatory changes, 41, 42, 74, 109, 124, 136
regulatory requirements, 82, 101, 109
reliability, 56, 70, 71, 101, 119, 135
requirements, vii, 1, 3, 5, 6, 7, 11, 13, 18, 19, 20, 21, 22, 23, 24, 25, 28, 29, 30, 31, 32, 35, 36, 37, 38, 40, 47, 50, 55, 56, 59, 61, 63, 66, 69, 82, 84, 85, 88, 95, 96, 100, 101, 105, 109, 112, 113, 117, 138
resources, 21, 45, 47, 48, 52, 62, 134
response, 5, 25, 31, 55, 81, 85, 101, 102, 104, 107, 113, 114, 115, 116
restrictions, 36, 99
restructuring, 138
retirement, 28, 115, 138
revenue, 3, 8, 12, 14, 21, 41, 42, 43, 47, 49, 50, 52, 66, 70, 72, 73, 76, 87, 88, 89, 91, 92, 94, 110, 112, 116, 119,

122, 126, 127, 128, 129, 130, 131, 137
risk, 3, 20, 22, 31, 39, 44, 51, 62, 103, 113, 126
rules, vii, 1, 3, 35, 36, 37, 39, 41, 45, 51, 53, 63, 67, 69, 75, 78, 79, 80, 86, 87, 91, 93, 95, 96, 98, 99, 100, 108, 110, 134, 135, 136, 137

S

savings, 2, 18, 25, 28, 29, 30
scope, 5, 6, 7, 28, 39, 56, 60, 70, 73, 90, 97, 118, 119, 120, 123, 134
segregation, 103, 106, 115
semi-structured interviews, 121, 123
services, 4, 7, 19, 20, 21, 22, 23, 27, 28, 29, 30, 33, 37, 38, 42, 43, 46, 48, 61, 62, 84, 95, 105, 134, 135, 138
shareholders, 4, 14, 95
SIC, 135, 140
Simplified Acquisition Procedures (SAP), 68, 77, 84, 136
Small Business Administration (SBA), i, iii, v, vii, 1, 2, 3, 4, 5, 6, 8, 9, 10, 11, 12, 13, 14, 18, 20, 21, 22, 30, 31, 32, 33, 35, 36, 37, 38, 39, 40, 41, 42, 43, 44, 45, 46, 47, 48, 49, 50, 51, 52, 53, 54, 55, 56, 57, 59, 61, 62, 63, 65, 66, 67, 68, 69, 70, 71, 72, 73, 74, 75, 76, 77, 78, 79, 80, 81, 82, 83, 84, 85, 86, 87, 88, 89, 90, 91, 92, 93, 94, 95, 96, 97, 98, 99, 100, 101, 102, 103, 104, 105, 106, 107, 108, 109, 110, 111, 112, 113, 114, 115, 116, 117, 118, 119, 120, 121, 122, 123, 126, 133, 134, 135, 136, 137, 138, 139, 140
Social Security Administration, 6, 26, 37, 53, 59
specialists, 53, 70, 77, 83, 84, 85, 92, 93, 100, 103, 104, 105, 106, 107, 109, 115, 116, 138
spending, 18, 62, 140
staffing, 67, 74, 100, 105, 106, 111, 115, 123, 138, 139
stakeholders, 104
state, 25, 31, 32, 33, 40, 41, 47, 48, 49, 55, 63, 66, 83, 86, 92, 94, 102, 103, 108, 111, 113
statutory provisions, 59
strategic planning, 92
structure, 7, 36, 48, 98, 103, 134, 139
style, 134, 139
succession, 111, 115, 139
support services, 23, 37, 42, 43, 46
surveillance, 62, 91, 92, 114, 116
System for Award Management (SAM), 68, 72, 119, 121, 122, 135, 139

T

target, 109
taxes, 99, 132
taxpayers, 25
technical assistance, 75, 77
technical change, 69, 136
technical comments, 54, 112
techniques, 25, 33, 92, 119
testing, 57, 119
time frame, 14, 19, 20, 53, 107, 109
Title I, 139
Title II, 139
total costs, 34
total revenue, 91, 122, 128, 129, 131
training, 30, 31, 74, 76, 82, 84, 85, 86, 102, 104, 110, 111, 113, 114, 115, 117, 138
transactions, 83, 102, 111, 115
transformations, 139
transition period, 47
Tribal 8(a) Firms, v, 1, 9, 14, 15, 16, 17, 18, 22, 45, 48, 50, 134
Tribal firms, vii, 1, 14, 51

U

U.S. General Services Administration (GSA), 3, 26, 67, 71, 135, 139, 140
unemployment rate, 11

United States, v, 1, 4, 65, 68
updating, 110, 114

V

variables, 72, 120, 135, 140
Voluntary Early Retirement Authority (VERA), 68, 105, 138
Voluntary Separation Incentive Payments (VSIP), 68, 105, 138
vulnerability, 88, 89, 91

W

wage rate, 34
wages, 28, 78
Washington, 6, 58, 59, 60, 61, 62, 63, 73, 98, 100, 123, 134, 135, 137, 138, 139
weakness, 49, 102
wildlife conservation, 133
withdrawal, 78, 96, 99, 100
workforce, 60, 74, 106, 116, 123
workload, 107
worldwide, 7, 134
written plans, 107, 116